Auditing Information Systems and Controls

Auditing Information Systems and Controls

The Only Thing Worse than
No Control is the Illusion of Control

Ed Danter

To order additional copies of this book, contact:
Xlibris
1-888-795-4274
www.Xlibris.com
Orders@Xlibris.com
575625

Contents

Part 1: Sarbanes Oxley and Regulatory Agencies

Part 2: Controls and IT Infrastructure

Part 3: The Audit Process

Part 4: Audit Activities

Part 5: New Challenges

To my wife Abby, who shared this journey with me from the beginning, who never stopped believing in me, who never allowed me to abandon hope and whose continuous inspiration, support and love helped me to achieve, what seemed at times, a never ending goal.

To my children and grandchildren, who by filling my life with happiness and joy flamed my enthusiasm. And to the memories of Judy Danter, who was always there for me, no matter how difficult the challenge and my dad, Harry Arnold, who instilled in me honesty and integrity.

Preface

The only thing worse than *no control*, is the *illusion* of control. If you believe there's no problem, you won't think about fixing it. Why spend the resources, time, effort, and cost to correct problems that don't exist? Having an illusion of control will encourage you to continue on the same course for months or years without any fear of being derailed. And when the train wreck becomes a reality, you'll wonder how it happened. You must avoid the illusion of control to survive.

In recent years, frequent headlines have exposed unethical corporate behavior, misleading accounting practices, and incompetent and illegal auditing processes. Companies such as Enron, Adelphi, Xerox, Arthur Anderson, ImClone, Tyco, and WorldCom, to name a few, have given us a glimpse into the misbehavior of some executives and made the public aware of inadequacies in corporate governance, and the potential risk. Corporate greed and malfeasance have resulted in criminal indictments of corporate executives for inflating earnings, falsifying financial statements, disguising company financial conditions, and misappropriating assets. Many CEOs' weak and inadequate leadership have resulted in the failure to detect shortcomings in control of business processes. This situation is compounded by some so-called external auditing professionals who have misled and deceived their clients—or conspired with them to deceive the public.

Corporate America is faced with a challenge today, a challenge unprecedented in our history. It has become a national imperative that corporations create programs and infrastructures to achieve audit readiness and guarantee the accuracy of corporate records. Executives should not and can not depend entirely on external audit reviews and recommendations. They must create internal audit programs and infrastructures to regain credibility and the confidence of shareholders. Meeting this challenge is critical to the survival and success of many business enterprises.

The federal government and leaders of our country are serious about facing the challenges and evolving dangers of corporate behavior, evidenced by the passing of the Sarbanes Oxley Act of 2002. The Act requires CEOs and CFOs to certify the accuracy of their financial statements, and mandates independent outside audit attestation of the operating effectiveness of controls and control structure over financial reporting. It imposes penalties for failure to comply. Pro-active corporations must establish the discipline of rigorous audit readiness programs and must ensure their continued successful execution. Internal audit committees must take measures to install checks and balances and self-policing practices to ensure integrity within their corporations. This is not optional. CEOs today are legally responsible for the correctness of their financial statements.

Today, corporate America is on shaky ground. The public's reaction is difficult to measure. Stock market performance is volatile and unpredictable, and there are countless instances of financial disappointment and loss. Corporations at risk must redeem credibility, pass external audits, and demonstrate strong controls to the satisfaction of government. They must also be able to stand up to public scrutiny.

The repercussions of fraudulent and inappropriate accounting and control practices can be widespread. The company's stockholders, creditors, and employees may suffer job loss and diminished retirement savings. Depositors in financial institutions, auditors, and accountants may be subject to investigations. Attorneys, insurers who write officers' liability policies and experience large claims, customers who depend on the company's products, merger companies who may enter into partnership based on erroneous finances, and even companies whose reputations can be tarnished by association, may all be affected.

It is critical that corporations regain a sense of ethical and honest behavior and return to basic effective corporate governance. As always, preventive and detective controls and adequate separation of duties need to be in place. It is vital that strong, solid, well executed audit programs be established to provide management teams with the necessary tools to restore trust and sound operations. Unfortunately, we can no longer put all of our faith in external audit organizations. Internal audit infrastructures must be the primary focus. Audit readiness emphasis needs to be placed on establishing ethical standards and expectations, education, behavior modification, preparation, and open and honest communications, and on the implementation of sound business practices and controls.

There is little doubt that when audit organizations are searching for essential business controls and auditability, they will be focusing on IT processes and controls, and they will be evaluating their effectiveness. Accurate financial statements and successful business processes are driven by and dependent upon the effectual implementation of solid, strong IT controls. Business functions are more closely integrated with IT controls than ever before. IT is the front end of business processes, the locomotive that powers the train. Most business functions today are either directly dependent on or are fed data from automated systems. The integrity of this data—that originates from IT systems and is reflected on a business statement and/or on a management report—is instrumental in driving important and sometimes critical business decisions. Its controls are essential to ensure that timely and accurate data is funneled to and digested by business processes. For businesses to disregard the importance of IT controls is as dangerous as ignoring the strength of a foundation when constructing a new house.

What This Book Covers

Auditing Information Systems and Controls: The Only Thing Worse Than No Control Is The Illusion of Control focuses on a new way to run a business, with a unique reporting structure and the formation of an internal independent audit organization. It proposes the establishment of an independent internal auditing group headed by a chief governance officer (CGO) or chief accounting executive (CAE) who reports directly to an audit committee, comprised of board of director members, who themselves must be totally independent. Independence is the most critical element in the success of this new audit approach and can not be emphasized enough. This will require an organizational change in most corporations and a revolutionary approach. Old paradigms in which the audit organization reported to the CEO or CFO will be discarded. These internal audit groups must serve as the eyes and ears of the public and board of directors. They will provide early warnings of inappropriate, fraudulent or ineffective practices and will report noncompliance with accepted basic control fundamentals and ethical behavior; they must do so without fear of reprisal.

Although I have seen many publications espousing the independence of a board of directors and the audit committee, the concept of a CGO/CAE who has governance responsibility and reports directly to the board of directors is somewhat unique. Not only is it the responsibility of the audit committee to provide direction, but it is essential that every executive officer and their staffs be on board and be fully supportive of the internal audit infrastructure. It is the synergy of these organizations working together that is required to prepare us for successful audits and to improve business controls.

Education is critical and should be of paramount importance in addressing this problem. Auditing Information Systems and Controls focuses on the establishment of effective corporate governance, describes how to install a sound audit governance infrastructure, and explains how to establish effective IT controls. This book not only addresses what is needed to comply with legislative mandates, but provides a roadmap, detailing steps on how to establish an infrastructure and audit readiness program to achieve compliance. In addition, there is a realization now by many corporations that the effectiveness of their business process controls is heavily dependent on the adequacy of their IT controls. This book educates current and future executives on the integration of business processes with IT controls.

This book is not confined to teaching audit fundamentals or explaining Sarbanes Oxley requirements. It combines these areas plus more. The book addresses many facets of IT controls, from the formation of an effective audit infrastructure and establishment of a controls framework, to today's challenges, including Sarbanes Oxley compliance where IT management has been outsourced. You will learn what controls need to be implemented, why they need to be implemented, and how best to put the most effective organization in place to ensure audit success. It is not enough to know what is required via Sarbanes Oxley legislation and other government regulations—you have to know how what controls need to be established and how to ensure that they are in place.

This book provides an educational foundation for the creation of an infrastructure to successfully address the auditing process, and enhance the process for ensuring audit quality. The infrastructure should help detect fraudulent activity, enhance the education of future participants responsible for controls, and position corporations to pass the scrutiny of external audits. This is not the ultimate answer to all corporate financial reporting and control problems, nor does it guarantee successful audits. It is not a panacea, but a starting point and building block for reviving faith in corporate America today, one that our leaders of tomorrow will find invaluable.

Controls have been mandated in today's corporate world, and this book helps you design a sound audit readiness program. It is a "common cent$" approach to controls. You want to be able to pass any audit, but not at the expense of profits. Control is a balance between business benefits and costs. Corporations have no choice but to have controlled environments, but there is latitude to select controls that will minimize complexity and installation costs while still achieving a sound control posture, and without exposing corporations to any additional risks.

This book supplies you with:

➢ Knowledge of why controls are needed.
➢ Consequences of not establishing adequate controls.
➢ The knowledge, skill and motivation to design and implement effective control and auditability features.
➢ Information on the synergy required of various organizations on control and auditability.
➢ The ability to choose an infrastructure that ensures effective controls.
➢ Understanding of the business impact and increased costs and risks resulting from inadequate controls, emphasizing Sarbanes Oxley legislature.

➤ Ability to assess the current state of your IT control environment.
➤ Understanding the need to maintain a balance between business needs and controls while establishing sound control posture.
➤ Help in efforts to design controls necessary to meet the IT directives of Sarbanes Oxley that will close the gaps between your current control environment and where you need to be.

In this book, I provide a streamlined approach, a roadmap that offers a step-by-step approach addressing development of control and auditability features, pro-active internal audits and the audit process.

I also address the responsibilities of various individuals and groups. This includes the board of directors, the audit committee, the chief auditing executive or chief governance officer, audit teams and current or future corporate executives. Not only is it the responsibility of the audit committee to provide direction, but it is essential that every executive officer and their staffs be on board and fully supportive of the internal audit infrastructure.

The book points out that those executives should not depend on external auditing firms, and should place the responsibility for audit readiness on the establishment of a completely independent internal audit infrastructure. There is a direct correlation between the thoroughness of the internal audit process and the readiness for an external audit.

This Book's Target Audience

Auditing Information Systems and Controls will benefit current and future corporate CEOs, CFOs, CIOs, boards of directors, and other executives who have or will have responsibility for ensuring that adequate controls are in place within their companies and that integrity and accuracy in financial reporting is achieved. Senior executives need to be well versed in internal control theory and practice to meet audit requirements. They must step up and enhance their knowledge of controls, understand their company's overall audit compliance plans, and ensure that the two are effectively integrated.

Corporations can use this book to instruct internal management on IT controls. *Auditing Information Systems and Controls* focuses on how to establish IT controls, how to integrate IT controls with business process controls, how executives can assess IT controls and how corporations can prepare for audit readiness compliance. With the recent trials, convictions, and sentencing of corporate executives, the demands for a sound IT control infrastructure become more important and essential for corporate America, with penalties for noncompliance being imposed. It is unacceptable for executives in today's corporate environment to be ignorant of IT controls.

This book particularly appeals to corporate management and their internal audit organizations where external organizations have been contracted to supply IT support, and where SAS70 reports are being requested for assessing control implementation and effective execution. This audience will grow as outsourcing expands; it is a rapidly evolving challenge. Compliance with Sarbanes Oxley in this environment is imposing unique demands both on professional auditing staffs and on corporate management.

Tomorrow's executives are an important audience. We need to focus education not only on the corporate executives of today but on the executives of tomorrow. And the time is now. The book could be a "primary source" used for teaching selective auditing, business controls, or corporate governance courses. Use it as an educational reference for various subjects, such as teaching the importance and necessity of IT controls, understanding audit fundamentals, establishing an auditing infrastructure, implementing control policies and processes, and understanding Sarbanes Oxley requirements.

Eventually, every business graduate student studying for his or her MBA should be required to take a basic course on controls and corporate governance. A basic knowledge of this topic is essential for every future corporate executive. IT controls are integrated into today's business processes and will play a significant role in business decisions in the years ahead.

How to Use This Book

Auditing Information Systems and Controls: is not meant to be an epochal discovery or to catapult corporate reporting to an idealistic summit. Its objective is simply to be an *educational reference*, to help us upright ourselves and put ourselves back on track. It is a book to be used by corporate executives who have, and will continue to have, what will seem to be a herculean mission at times: the resurrection of public faith in corporate America.

This book covers a broad scope, from the "why's" and "what's" of Sarbanes Oxley, to the establishment of the infrastructure and IT controls necessary for audit survival, to the audit process used by external auditors. Focus will be on addressing the "how to" efforts for the implementation of effective control activities.

This book need not be read in order, cover-to-cover; feel free to browse among the chapters and topics of particular relevance to you. I include case studies and real-life examples from my more than 20 years of audit experience (both as an auditee and auditor). I have worked for IBM for more than 35 years, and I am grateful for the opportunities that allowed me to enhance my audit experience and education. However, the opinions in this book are mine and do not necessarily reflect the opinions or positions of IBM.

Chapter One

Sarbanes Oxley Highlights

"The wish to acquire more is admittedly a very natural and common thing; and when men succeed in this they are always praised rather than condemned. But when they lack the ability to do so and yet want to acquire more at all costs, they deserve condemnation for their mistakes."

—Niccolo Machiavelli

Introduction

As a result of corporate financial scandals that plagued corporate America in recent years, Congress passed the Sarbanes-Oxley Act of 2002, also known as the Public Company Accounting Reform and Investor Protection Act of 2002 and frequently referred to as SOX, to build and restore confidence in public financial reporting.

SOX includes issues such as establishing a public accounting oversight board (PCAOB), auditor independence, corporate responsibility and enhanced financial disclosure. The Act requires the certification by CEOs and CFOs regarding the accuracy of their financial statements and requires independent outside audit attestation of the operating effectiveness of controls and control structure over financial reporting. It imposes associated penalties for failure to comply.

It is considered one of the most significant changes to United States securities laws since the New Deal in the 1930s. The Act grants additional powers and responsibilities to the U.S. Securities and Exchange Commission for regular reviews and enforcement. SOX legislature is a framework with SEC rules providing the details through the Public Company Accounting Oversight Board (PCAOB).

Is Sarbanes Oxley more effective than past legislature, and is it a deterrent that would have prevented any of the financial scandals that we have been subjected to over the last few years? We may not be where we ideally would like to with the legislature being an absolute deterrent against fraudulent behavior or erroneous financial reporting, but we are certainly on the right track. Examples of situations where there were indictments as a result of SOX legislature, and instances where there were punitive actions taken are:

July 28, 2005—A federal jury in Birmingham Alabama found Richard Scrushy, HealthSouth Corporation founder, not guilty of securities fraud, conspiracy and violating the Sarbanes Oxley Act of 2002. However, the SEC is requesting repayment of ill-gotten gains, seeking civil penalties, and asking the Birmingham federal court to bar Scrushy from being an officer or director in any public company.

January 27, 2005—Thomas Trauger, a former audit partner in Earnst & Young, was sentenced to 12 months in federal prison, ordered to pay a $5,000 fine, and undergo two years of supervised release for his part in altering and falsifying accounting records with the intent to impede a federal investigation. Earlier, on October 29, 2004, Thomas Trauger had pleaded guilty to falsifying records in a federal investigation in violation of the Sarbanes-Oxley Act. He admitted as part of this plea that he knowingly altered, destroyed and falsified records with the intent to impede and obstruct an investigation by the Securities and Exchange Commission (SEC). This is one of the first cases of document destruction brought under the recently enacted Sarbanes-Oxley Act.

December 25, 2005—Enron's former chief accountant Richard Causey pled guilty as part of a plea bargain. Thirty-two charges were brought against Causey for fraud, conspiracy, and lying to auditors.

January 24, 2005—Andrew Fastow, chief financial officer for Enron, pleaded guilty to two counts of wire and securities fraud and agreed to serve a 10-year prison sentence.

October 24, 2006—Jeffrey Skilling, ex-Enron Chief Executive Officer, was sentenced to 24 years and 4 months in prison for fraud and inside trading. The charges stated that Skilling used various devices and schemes to manipulate Enron's financial results from 1999 to 2001. Ken Lay, Enron founder, found guilty along with Jeffrey Skilling, died on July 5, 2006, before sentencing.

In time, SOX will be an even more effective deterrent. As fines and jail sentences increase, so will SOX effectiveness. A significant number of corporations are presently scrambling to put control infrastructures in place to be able to comply with SOX legislature. There is justified concern on the part of many CEOs and CFOs of not being compliant. They will need to establish and ensure effective execution of internal control infrastructures to avoid possible punitive action with hefty fines and jail sentences. They will need to be 'audit ready' with potentially significant cost and efforts required in many cases, to pass external audits. This is a daunting task and an impressive challenge that is being turned down by many CFOs. The turnover of CFOs among leading corporations is higher than ever before. They do not want to fail, and more and more frequently are bailing out. Many CFOs are changing companies to avoid the challenge, which must appear Herculean at times, with little chance of winning and a real threat of losing everything. In some instances they are even changing career paths.

In "New Regulations Continue to Drive CFO Recruitment," an article by Suzanne McGee that appeared in the Wall Street Journal Executive Career site, she states "The Sarbanes-Oxley Act of 2002 is reshaping the corporate world, but nowhere is it having a greater impact than within the offices of chief financial officers. Nationwide, companies of all sizes are demanding more from their chief financial officers and expanding the ranks of other finance executives to help them carry the ever-growing auditing and accounting burden. Larger businesses are adding the position of chief compliance officer to tackle the specific issues required by Sarbanes-Oxley, particularly the creation and oversight of new financial controls."

In this chapter I will give highlights of the Sarbanes-Oxley legislature to provide an overview of its expectations and demands that have lead some corporations, audit committees and chief executives to be concerned with compliance and the necessity of changing their audit infrastructures.

Background

As a result of the corporate scandals of the 1990's (e.g. Enron, Tyco, Worldcom, now MCI), Congress passed the Sarbanes Oxley Act. It was approved by the House by a vote of 423-3 and by the senate by a unanimous vote of 99-0. It was signed into law on July 30, 2002 by President George W. Bush. The sponsors of the law, after which it is named, were Paul Sarbanes, a Democratic representative from Maryland, and Michael Oxley, a Republican from Ohio. The act was put into law to protect investors by improving the accuracy and reliability of corporate disclosures. The act includes issues such as establishing a public accounting oversight board (PCAOB), auditor independence, corporate responsibility and enhanced financial disclosure.

It is important to realize that although the Sarbanes Oxley Act places responsibility on the CEO and CFO for the accuracy of their financial statements, and we will see this below, SOX recognized that IT plays an important role. The PCAOB was aware of the significant role that IT systems have in generating accurate information and reporting data and the fact that IT processes are integrated with business processes to such an extent that they place a large responsibility on the CIO. They realized that the reliability of financial reporting is heavily dependent on a well-controlled IT environment. The PCAOB made this evident in Auditing Standard No 2. They stated, "The nature and characteristics of a company's use of information technology in its information system affect the company's internal control over financial reporting."

The following definitions of Section 302 and Section 404 (as well as additional pertinent information on these two standards) were extracted from "IT Control Objectives for Sarbanes-Oxley—The Importance of IT in the Design, Implementation and Sustainability of Internal Control Over Disclosure and Financial Reporting" produced by the IT Governance Institute in 2004. This extract is very informative and helpful in understanding PCAOB objectives and the intent of Sarbanes Oxley relative to IT controls:

> "The PCAOB standard includes specific requirements for auditors to understand the flow of transactions, including how transactions are initiated, authorized, recorded, processed and reported. Such transactions' flows commonly involve the use of application systems for automating processes and supporting high volume and complex

transaction processing. The reliability of these application systems is in turn reliant upon various IT support systems, including networks, databases, operating systems and more. Collectively, they define the IT systems that are involved in the financial reporting process and, as a result, should be considered in the design and evaluation of internal control.

The PCAOB suggests that these IT controls have a pervasive effect on the achievement of many control objectives. They also provide guidance on the controls that should be considered in evaluating an organizations' internal control, including program development, program changes, computer operations, and access to programs and data. While general in nature, these PCAOB principles provide direction on where SEC registrants likely should focus their efforts to determine whether specific IT controls over transactions are properly designed and operating effectively."

The PCAOB states that when we talk about internal control it is important to realize that one size does not fit all, and that controls should be designed to match the size and complexity of the company.

It is also essential for executive management to understand that there is no certitude that the design of reasonable controls will guarantee the accuracy and reliability of IT processing and subsequent financial reporting, as the human factor always plays a significant role. The achievement of a company's control objectives is limited by manual decision making, possible collusion by two or more parties, and circumvention and override of inherent controls. However, a sound control infrastructure will improve the odds of effectiveness, reliability, and dependability.

Let us take a closer look at the Sarbanes Oxley Act. The SEC mandates the use of an internal control framework, and SOX encourages the use of COSO or a similar framework.

SOX applies to companies traded on the US exchanges with market value greater than $75 million. This was effective for fiscal years ending after June 15, 2004 with the compliance of smaller companies required as of the first fiscal year ending on or after June 15, 2005. However it is widely expected that other securities regulators will issue regulations that are in the spirit of Sarbanes Oxley. There are also efforts by foreign companies, not on the US exchanges, to be proactive and adopt SOX philosophies. Although private companies do not need to comply with SOX, they must be in compliance prior to issuing any stock or debt or selling a significant shareholding to a public company.

Compliance with SOX will result in improved corporate accountability, should reduce fraudulent opportunities, should keep CEO's and CFO's out of jail and reduce exposure to payment of substantial fines. However, it should also be a catalyst for improved quality of business processing and enhance the accuracy of financial reporting. Past SEC chairman, William Donaldson remarked, "Simply complying with the rules is not enough. They should as I have said before, make this approach part of their companies' DNA. For companies that take this approach, most of the major concerns about compliance disappear. Moreover, if companies view the new laws as opportunities—opportunities to improve internal controls, improve the performance of the board, and improve their public reporting—they will ultimately be better run, more transparent, and therefore more attractive to investors."

When we review Sarbanes Oxley with an IT perspective, we need to focus on SOX sections 302 and 404, especially section 404 where IT requirements are specifically addressed.

Section 302

Section 302 went into effect in July 2002. It requires a company's management, with the participation of the principal executive and financial officers (the certifying officers), to make the following quarterly and annual certifications with respect to the company's internal control over financial reporting:

> ➢ A statement that the certifying officers are responsible for establishing and maintaining internal control over financial reporting
> ➢ A statement that the certifying officers have designed such internal control over financial reporting, or caused such internal control over financial reporting to be designed under their supervision, to provide reasonable assurance regarding the reliability of financial reporting and the preparation of financial statements for external purposes in accordance with generally accepted accounting principles
> ➢ A statement that the report discloses any changes in the company's internal control over financial reporting that occurred during the most recent fiscal quarter (the company's fourth fiscal quarter in the case of an annual report) that have materially affected, or are reasonably likely to materially affect, the company's internal control over financial reporting.

Section 404

Section 404 went into effect in the year-ends beginning on or after November 15, 2004. Foreign security registrants had until November 2005 to be compliant.

The directives of Sarbanes-Oxley section 404 require that management provide an annual report on its assessment of internal control over financial reporting in the annual filing. It states:

> Management's report on internal control over financial reporting is required to include the following:

> ➢ A statement of management's responsibility for establishing and maintaining adequate internal control over financial reporting for the company

> ➢ A statement identifying the framework used by management to conduct the required assessment of the effectiveness of the company's internal control over the financial reporting

> ➢ An assessment of the effectiveness of the company's internal control over financial reporting as of the end of the company's most recent fiscal year, including an explicit statement as to whether that internal control over financial reporting is effective

> ➢ A statement that the registered public accounting firm that audited the financial statements included in the annual report has issued an attestation report on management's assessment of the company's internal control over financial reporting

It is important to note that the significance of Section 404 is not only that it requires senior management to establish and maintain an adequate internal controls structure, but that it also requires senior management to annually assess their effectiveness, as stated above. This is where the necessity of a sound internal control infrastructure is of paramount importance.

Once senior management has annually assessed control effectiveness, Section 404 requires that a company's external auditors *attest* to management's assessment of management's control assessment of its internal controls, including IT controls. Management must be able to provide their external auditors with evidence of functional controls and documentation of test results that resulted in their assessment. SOX legislature precludes management from concluding that internal controls are effective if there are any material weaknesses, and requires management to identify all material weaknesses. External auditors will then have the option of accepting your test results after their review for their attestation, or they can opt to conduct their own testing before their attestation is finalized. If the external auditors opt to do their own testing, which is very likely, they will probably meet with senior management to determine the time period being audited. The attestation of effective controls is not confined to a specific date but it applies to a reasonably agreed to time period. This is usually between a six-month and 12-month period. At the end of the most current fiscal year, management's annual reports must be filed with the SEC.

When your external auditors look at your IT control infrastructure, they will be looking at:

➤ Information management
➤ Data classification
➤ Authentication, initiation and authorization of transactions
➤ Transaction thresholds and tolerance levels
➤ Data processing integrity and accuracy

In addition, external auditors will focus on identification of risks related to IT systems and the mitigation of these risks for continued effectiveness.

Other SOX Standards

➤ Section 303: Audit Partner Rotation
The lead audit or coordinating partner and the reviewing partner must rotate every five years

➤ Section 206: Conflict of Interest
The CEO, Controller, Chief Accounting Officer or person in equivalent position cannot have been employed by the company's audit firm during the one-year period preceding the audit.

➤ Section 301: Public
Each member of the audit committee shall be a member of the board of directors if the issuer, and shall otherwise be independent. "Independent" means not having received fees for any consulting, advisory or other compensation fee from the company or working for the company or any subsidiary other than for services on the board.

➤ Section 404: Management Assessment of Internal Controls
In addition to the annual assessment by management and attestation by the external auditors as to the effectiveness of the internal control structure as indicated above, each company must adopt a code of ethics for its senior financial officers and reveal the contents of that code.

➤ Section 407: Disclosure of Audit Committee Financial Expert
At least one member of the audit committee must be a 'financial expert."

➤ Title IX: White Collar Penalty Enhancements
If financial statements are not filed with the SEC that are certified by the CEO and CFO that indicate that there is full compliance with Sarbanes Oxley, fines and imprisonment can be imposed. The maximum penalty is $500,000 and/or imprisonment of up to five years.

➤ Section 1102: Tampering with a Record or Otherwise Impeding an Official Process
It is a crime for any person to corruptly alter, destroy, mutilate or conceal any document with the intent to impair the objects' integrity or availability for official use.

When outside auditing firms have been commissioned to attest to the effectiveness of your internal control infrastructure, they will be using the control structure that you provide them with. They will, on many occasions, be more thorough than you could have ever imagined. Sarbanes Oxley has certainly raised the bar. In the past, their audit reports were generated and distributed to your audit committee, but SOX places a new responsibility and burden on them, with their reports being submitted to the SEC. The audit firms are being held accountable for the accuracy of their reports and will take extreme caution before they attest to the accuracy of controls and their effectives with their signatures. Their reputations are on the line as well as the reputation of your corporation. This book will focus on compliance to sections 302 and 404. I do not mean to minimize the importance of the other sections that I mentioned but the meat of Auditing Information Systems and Controls stems from compliance with sections 302 and 404.

Summary

As a result of the corporate scandals that surfaced, much more frequently than the public would have ever thought possible, and the need to restore faith in corporate reporting, the federal government passed the Sarbanes Oxley Act in the summer of 2002. This is one of the most powerful financial legislatures that America has seen in more than fifty years, with expanded governance regulations and the strong possibility of heavy penalties and incarceration being inflicted for noncompliance. There has been recent evidence of indictments and subsequent sentencing due to fraudulent behavior and noncompliance, and we will probably see more punitive action taken in the months and years ahead. The focus of Auditing Information Systems and Controls rests on SOX sections 302 and 404. In section 302, management must certify that they have a sound internal controls infrastructure in place. In section 404, management must not only confirm that their controls are effective but in addition an outside independent audit firm must attest to the effectiveness of execution. The PCAOB, established by the Sarbanes Oxley Act, recommends that the COSO framework be used, but other frameworks can be used if they are comparatively effective. Because of the dependence of business and financial reporting on IT, it is imperative that not only CEOs and CFOs be familiar with SOX legislature but that CIOs understand SOX requirements for compliance and the ramification of noncompliance as well.

Chapter Two

Regulatory Agencies and Control Frameworks

"The fish sees the bait, not the hook; a person sees the gain, not the danger."

—Chinese proverb

Introduction

Have you ever sat with your managers, executives, future executives, colleagues, neighbors, or friends and wondered where the controls were before Sarbanes Oxley? Didn't we have any legislature in this country that would have prevented, or at least discouraged, the corporate scandals that we were plagued with in the last few years?

IT governance did not spring from the head of Zeus, nor was it born with Sarbanes Oxley. There is a history that preceded Sarbanes Oxley, before the corporate scandals that have surfaced over the last few years. The scandals of Enron, Worldcom, Tyco, HealthSouth, and others were the catalysts for SOX legislature that reinforced previous legislature and gave it teeth. I think it is important for the reader not only to be somewhat familiar with earlier legislature but also to be aware of the control frameworks that existed prior to SOX and are endorsed by it. My intent is not to go into depth on this subject, as the reader can certainly follow up on his or her own. My objective is to enlighten the reader about the existence of control governance and frameworks.

Sarbanes Oxley (SOX) doesn't mark the first attempt to improve the audit process. During the 1970s, '80s, and '90s, a series of commissions—the Cohen Commission in 1978, the Treadway Commission in 1985, the Jenkins Committee in 1994, the Committee of Sponsoring Organizations in 1999, and the Panel on Audit Effectiveness of the Public Oversight Board, or POB in 2000—issued reports recommending changes. There might have been other commissions and I don't intend to include them all, but to give a flavor of regulatory efforts that produced guidance that preceded Sarbanes Oxley. Below are timelines, before and after SOX, of some of these significant activities, the various organizations involved, and a brief description.

Timeline for Regulatory Commissions and Frameworks before SOX

There was regulatory activity and guidance that preceded Sarbanes Oxley. For example:

SEC	ISACA	FCPA	Cohen Commission Rpt	COSO framework	COBIT	Jenkins Committee Rpt	COSO Fraud Rpt	POB
1934	1969	1977	1978	1985	1990's	1994	1999	2000

1934—Establishment of the Security and Exchange Commissions (SEC).

1969—ISACA, the Institute of Systems Audit and Control Association, was established and subsequently generated standards, guidelines and procedures over the years.

1977—Congress passed the Foreign Corrupt Practices Act.

1978—The Cohen Commission, appointed by the American Institute of Certified Public Accounts (AICPA), generated a report on the responsibilities of independent auditors.

1985—The Treadway Commission issued the COSO (Committee of Sponsoring Organizations) framework.

Early 1990's—The IT Governance Institute created COBIT (Control Objectives for Informational related Technology).

1994—The AICPA released the executive summary of its special committee, better known as the Jenkins Committee on financial reporting.

1999—The Committee of Sponsoring Organizations of the Treadway Commission (COSO) issued a report after analysis of financial statement occurrences.

2000—The Public Oversight Board appointed a Panel on Audit Effectiveness that released a report that found audit quality fundamentally sound.

SEC

Following the stock market crash and passage of the Securities Act of 1933, that states that investors are to receive financial and other significant information concerning securities being offered for public sale, Congress passed the Securities and Exchange Act of 1934. This act established the Securities and Exchange Commission to enforce the newly passed securities laws, monitor the securities industry, promote stability in the markets and, most importantly, protect investors.

The SEC requires public companies to disclose meaningful financial and other information to the public. The intent is to provide knowledge for all investors to use to judge for themselves whether to buy, sell, or hold a particular security. Congress felt that only through the steady flow of timely, comprehensive, and accurate information can people make sound investment decisions.

ISACA

ISACA is one of today's most influential and well established organizations. With more than 35,000 members in over 100 countries, the *Information Systems Audit and Control Association* (ISACA) is a recognized global leader in IT governance, control, and assurance. Founded in 1969, ISACA sponsors international conferences, administers the globally respected CISA (Certified Information Systems Auditor) designation, and develops globally applicable information systems (IS) auditing and control standards.

Foreign Corrupt Practices Act

The Foreign Corrupt Practices Act of 1977 laid down some fundamentals more than a quarter of a century ago. It stated, "Reporting companies are required to devise and maintain a system of internal accounting controls sufficient to provide reasonable assurances that:

➢ Transactions are executed in accordance with management's general or specific authorization.
➢ Transactions are recorded as necessary to:
  • Permit preparation of financial statements in conformity with generally accepted accounting principles or any other criteria applicable to such statements and
  • Maintain accountability for its assets.
➢ Access to assets is permitted only in accordance with management's general or specific authorization.
➢ The recorded accountability for its assets is compared with existing assets at reasonable intervals and appropriate action is taken with respect to any differences."

AICPA (Cohen Commission)

Another institution that has played a significant role over many years in raising the bar for auditors is the American Institute of Certified Public Accounts (AICPA). The AICPA appointed the Cohen commission that met from 1974 until 1978 when they issued their report. The commission was charged with the task of developing conclusions and recommendations regarding the responsibilities of independent auditors. What is important to note is that in their conclusion they stated that a gap existed between the performance of the auditors and expectations of the financial community.

COSO

You can't talk to many IT personnel about Sarbanes Oxley without talking about COSO (the Committee of Sponsoring Organizations). COSO is a voluntary private sector organization dedicated to improving the quality of financial reporting through business ethics, effective internal control, and corporate governance. It was originally formed in 1985 by the National Commission on Fraudulent Financial Reporting and studied the casual factors that can lead to fraudulent financial reporting, developing recommendations for public companies and their independent auditors, for the SEC and for educational institutions. The Chairman of the National Commission was James Treadway, Jr. a former commissioner of the SEC, hence the commonly referred to name of the Treadway Commission.

The COSO control framework is recommended by Sarbanes Oxley and is recognized as the standard framework to be adopted by public companies.

There are 5 components under the COSO Framework. They are:

➢ Control Environment
➢ Information and Communication
➢ Control Activities
➢ Monitoring
➢ Risk Assessment

Control Environment

The control environment is where it all begins. It establishes the foundation for all other components of internal control, providing discipline and structure. Control environment factors include the ethics, values, and direction established by the executives and disseminated through management with assigned responsibilities and authority.

Information and Communications

Information must be identified and distributed throughout a company in such a way that people perform their responsibilities effectively. This information can be IT generated reports containing financial and operational information. It needs to be accurate and timely. In addition, there needs to be effective communication from executives down throughout the corporation giving employees a sense of support for their efforts and clear understanding of their responsibilities and the effect of their control activities on others. In addition to effective internal communications there needs to be effective external communication with suppliers, customers, and external auditors.

Control Activities

These are the policies, processes, and procedures that help ensure that personnel can execute management directives. These control activities are important al all levels within a corporation from the top executives, through management, to the individual in the organization performing a control task. They should address, at the minimum, security of access, separation of duties, reconciliations, reviews, approvals, and authorizations.

Monitoring

It is essential to monitor performance over whether controls are working as effectively as designed. It is necessary to ensure that quality is maintained. If monitoring discloses shortcomings or degradation in quality, the control activities will need to be reviewed and possibly modified.

Risk Assessment

Internal as well as external risks need to be assessed. The assessments should identify how the risks should be managed. Corporations also need to identify and deal with risks as a result of environmental or business change.

It is important to realize that there is a strong link and interrelationship among the five components that form the basis for a strong control framework. All components must be functioning effectively for internal control to be effective. This is truly an integrated framework where the direction, support, execution, and realization of the importance of what needs to be accomplished and the risks involved need to be effective over time, regardless of change.

COBIT

COSO and COBIT (Control Objectives for Information and Related Technology) although not inseparable are closely related. COBIT produced a high level and detailed set of control objectives for IT Management. COSO references COBIT as a good proactive source for IT governance.

COBIT defines IT control objectives based on a library of books that documents best practices for IT service management (ITIL). The control objectives are included under four domains:

- ➤ Planning and organization
- ➤ Delivery and support processes
- ➤ Acquisition and implementation and
- ➤ Monitoring processes.

There are twelve Cobit based control objectives that align with the four domains and closely support PCAOB principles that external auditors will probably focus on. These are:

1. Application software
2. Technology infrastructure
3. Developing and maintaining policies and procedures
4. Testing of application software
5. Change Management
6. Service Level Management
7. Third—party services
8. Systems security
9. Configuration Management
10. Problem Management
11. Data management
12. Operations Management

We will be taking a closer look at most of these objectives throughout *Auditing Information Systems and Controls.*

AICPA (Jenkins Committee)

In 1994 the AICPA released the executive summary of a report submitted by its Special Committee on Financial Reporting. This committee was known as the Jenkins Committee after its chairman Edward Jenkins. The committee was established to study the relevance of business reporting standards. It recommended increased disclosure of business unit activities and better accounting standards.

COSO Fraud Report

In the summer of 1999, research commissioned by COSO of the Treadway Commission provided a report on analysis of financial statements of fraudulent related occurrences. One of the primary objectives of the commission was to examine key company and management characteristics of the companies involved in instances of financial statement fraud. The commission found that more than half of the frauds involved overstating revenues by recording revenues prematurely or fictitiously. The commission pointed out the importance of interim reviews of quarterly financial statements and the benefits of continuous auditing.

POB Report on Audit Effectiveness

Again, going back more than twenty-five years, the Public Oversight Board (POB) was created in 1977 as an independent private sector body, commissioned to oversee and report on the programs of the SECPS (SEC Practice Section). In the summer of 2000 a panel of the POB examining audit effectiveness, found that audit quality was fundamentally sound. In May of 2002, as a result of their own recommendation, the POB was terminated, to be replaced by a more effective oversight body. The new organization was the PCAOB (Public Company Account Oversight Board), created by the Sarbanes Oxley Act.

Timeline for Regulatory Legislature from SOX going forward

SOX	Audit Standard #2	Basel II Accord
2002	2004	2004

It is of course necessary to look at the legislation from Sarbanes Oxley going forward. Chapter One is dedicated exclusively to Sarbanes Oxley and its provisions that impact IT corporate governance. A brief description of the legislature depicted in the timeline above follows.

2002—Congress passed the Sarbanes Oxley Act, which gave additional governance powers to the SEC, and created the Public Company Accounting Oversight Board (PCAOB). Details are discussed in Chapter One.

March 9, 2004—The Public Company Accounting Oversight Board (PCAOB) issued Audit Standard #2, an IT regulation, which was endorsed by the SEC.

June 2004—The Basel Committee passed the Basel II Accord that imposed strict regulations on the banking community.

SOX Highlights

SOX had as its foundation the commissions and framework which preceded it—but it gave teeth and more bite to regulatory governance. SOX imposed heavy punitive damages to non compliance in the way of large fines and incarceration. It is regarded by many as probably is the most significant financial control legislature in the last fifty years. Details of the SOX Act were discussed in the previous chapter.

Audit Standard #2

The POB was no longer in existence after May 2002, and the Sarbanes Oxley Act recognized a void that needed to be filled. The Sarbanes Oxley Act of 2002 created the PCAOB, a private sector, non-profit organization, to oversee the auditors of public companies in order to protect the interests of investors and further the public interest in the preparation of informative, fair, and independent audit reports. The PCAOB believed that more clarification and guidance was needed for companies to be able to comply with SOX section 404.

Standard No. 2 is the standard on attestation engagements refereed to in Section 404(b) as well as Section 103(a) (2) (A) of the Sarbanes—Oxley Act of 2002. The Board submitted this standard to the Securities and Exchange Commission (SEC) and it was subsequently approved on March 9, 2004.

Audit Standard No. 2, also referred to as the "March 9 document" makes the point that management is required to base its assessment of the company's internal control over financial reporting on a suitable recognized control framework, established by a body of experts following due-process procedures. The Board states that COSO provides a suitable framework for purposes of management's assessment. The board also states that other frameworks may have been published in countries outside of the US or might be published in the future. Regardless, any framework should have elements that encompass all of COSO's general themes. Whether using COSO or another suitable framework, the auditor should apply the concepts and guidance in Auditing Standard No. 2 in a reasonable manner.

Important points that Standard No. 2 addresses are:

➢ The board of directors, and not the independent auditor, is responsible for evaluating the effectiveness of the audit committee.
➢ The independent auditor should consider the effectiveness of the audit committee.
➢ The independent auditor's own work must be the source of providing evidence for its opinions.
➢ The independent auditor is to evaluate management's assessment process to determine whether management has a basis for reaching its conclusion.
➢ The auditor needs to test the effectiveness of internal control to be satisfied that management's conclusion is correct.

Basel II Accord

The Basel Committee, which was established by the Bank of International Settlements, produced the first Basel Accord in 1988 that established a set of rules and regulations focused on international banks. In June of 2004, the Basel Committee modified Basel Accord I and released the Basel Accord II. The rational for the new accord was to address the need for a system of controls that extended the scope of Basel Accord I to operational risks.

The Basel II Accord understands that in order to put trust in business processes to capture appropriate data, analyze the data, and draw conclusions for the business, they will need to heavily depend on IT processing. The Basel Commission put demands on IT departments for data collection, analysis, reporting, and storage. They also understood that IT infrastructure must be sound and a limited operational risk. The Basel Commission recognized the strong dependency of businesses on IT processing.

The operational risk that Basel II Accord addresses is the risk to the business of direct or indirect business loss resulting from inadequate or failed internal processes, people, and systems, or from external events. Basel Accord II placed a major dependency on IT to reduce risk, and focused on reviewing how IT is used to collect, analyze, and report data that quantifies the control needed to protect the banks. Basel II Accord emphasized the linkage between technology and business. The Basel II Accord integrates business controls with IT controls, and reinforces the control frameworks proposed and referenced by Sarbanes Oxley.

There is a significant Basel thrust on security, and security controls, as there should be in the banking industry. When we talk about operational controls in a later chapter, we will be addressing security controls. The stronger the security controls, the smaller the risk of inappropriate and fraudulent access to data. Reduction of risk is a necessity and certainly an objective of both Basel II Accord and SOX legislature. In addition to system access, and operational risk identification, Basel II realizes the importance of data integrity, business continuity, measurements, and reporting, which are covered in subsequent chapters.

Basel II Accord realized that a business generally evolves more quickly than its IT infrastructure, and financial institutions need to assure themselves that IT is flexible enough and adequately controlled to met business demands. The other important point Basel II Accord makes is that there needs to be a heavy investment in IT infrastructure to provide adequate control environments for cost reduction and productivity improvements. Mature IT infrastructures and effective control frameworks will reduce business risks and improve processing quality.

Basel II addresses large international bank operations and focuses on reducing risks while improving capital and profits. Naturally, IT plays an important role here, especially in an outsourcing environment where banks are looking to reduce risks and exposures. The focus of the Basel II Accord is on banking processes, but the commission realized that IT processes and controls play a significant role and that the banking and IT worlds need to be integrated from a controls perspective. You can not separate Basel II requirements from SOX compliance; we are talking about corporate governance as it extends into the banking community.

Summary

Federal regulations have been on the books for more than a quarter of a century addressing control fundamentals, control frameworks, and governance responsibilities, as well as external auditor roles that should protect the public from erroneous and fraudulent financial reporting. Numerous agencies have been established to review and recommend improvements over the years. We have had the establishment of ISACA, the AICPA, POB, and PCAOB, and numerous commissions put in place by these organizations to review and report on effectiveness of corporate governance. However, none were effective enough to deter the corporate scandals that we have been subjected to in the last few years. As a result the SEC fully endorsed the Sarbanes Oxley Act of 2002 which gave considerable teeth to our legislature and threatened to impose heavy fines and jail sentences to the CEOs and CFOs of the corporations in violation of the new law.

The importance of external oversight of financial controls can not be minimized. On January 24, 2003 the SEC voted to adapt rules that would require lawyers to take concerns about violations of security laws to top executives at a company they advise and if necessary to corporate boards. The SEC also has mandated that every CEO is responsible to attest to the accuracy of their financial reporting or suffer legal consequences.

Chapter Three

Controls Overview

"The only thing worse than no control is the illusion of control."

—Anonymous

Introduction

As CEO, should you be concerned about an "illusion of control"? Imagine yourself in this scenario and think how you would react:

It's Tuesday, March 14, and you are sitting having your coffee, skimming your messages on your PC, when John Walker, your VP of operations, and Sally Boker, your VP of application programming, walk into your office. As CEO you have just been informed by your auditing partners that they are announcing an IT audit, and you requested John and Sally to come to your office. You ask them if they are ready for the audit or if you should try to postpone it to allow them ample preparation time. They have no intention of appearing unready, and tell you that you can invite the auditors in. They assure you that they have faith in their audit posture and that they will not let you down. They inform you that their controls are strong, sound, and well established. They acknowledge that they might have a few weaknesses but that fundamentally their organizations have controls in place that are executing well enough to pass the external audit that was just announced. You ask them how they arrived at this conclusion. They respond without hesitation and with confidence that they were informed of their control posture by their management teams, who are paid to know if controls are in place or not. They are ready and there is nothing to worry about; they are in excellent positions to pass any audit.

They spend the next two weeks before the audit commencement establishing liaisons and planning logistics that will make the auditors as comfortable as possible. They have arranged for a plush conference room, individual offices for each auditor, breakfast and lunches catered in every day, have made sure that the auditors will have a full cabinet of supplies at their disposal and connectivity for their PCs. But your organizations are completely unprepared for the audit and don't even know it. It is reminiscent of the emperor's new clothes. The pig is about to be slaughtered; there is no advance warning. Much to your chagrin, one of your worst nightmares is soon to take place and it will take you completely by surprise.

April 21st arrives and you are invited to attend an audit summary meeting along with John and Sally. You can't believe the results, one of the most devastating audits that you have ever been hit with, a total disaster and shockingly unsatisfactory. After the auditors leave, you turn toward John and Sally. You say to them that it appears they had an illusion of control, which was worse than having no control at all because the latter could have and would have been addressed, *before* the auditors arrived. You advise them that you are an unhappy camper and that immediate action will be taken in addition to compensation repercussions that they should expect. You have hired an outside audit consultant who will immediately establish executive management awareness classes that they must attend. They will learn the importance and benefits of controls and basic control philosophy. They should never again assume that they have stellar audit readiness programs or even satisfactory control positions without thoroughly reviewing and validating the control opinions and assessments of their management teams. You are mandating that they attend these classes along with their management teams so that they never again have "an illusion of control." It would be better if they knew where their weaknesses were and what controls they did not have so they could fix the exposures, rather than be unaware of problems and assume everything is all right. The end result is a false comfort level and conviction that there is no need to establish corrective plans for fixing anything. Why fix something if you believe it isn't broken? The only thing worse than no control, is the illusion of control. How true that statement is, how true.

In this chapter we will be looking at the importance of controls, control axioms, benefits of sound IT controls, and control principles.

Importance of Controls

IT controls is not a new concept, nor was it created as a result of federal legislature. It did not just arrive on the scene; it has been around for decades. However, it is now in the spotlight with the importance of controls never having been greater.

Every corporate executive, or future corporate executive, should realize that controls have always been important, and have not resulted from the emergence of the Sarbanes Oxley Act. Throughout the last few years, it seems everyone's concern has been elevated, with controls becoming an integral part of the immediate strategic plans in many corporations. You can even hear controls being discussed around the water coolers in the office. Controls are no longer as much an afterthought as they were in the design and in the development of new applications nor when planning application maintenance and IT operational support. The audits conducted by external audit organization are much more thorough and demanding then they ever have been in the past. There are numerous reasons why your IT environment must contain adequate control and auditability features. I have listed some of these below:

> ➤ One of the most detrimental results of inadequate controls to a company is the revenue loss resulting from IT inadequacies in correcting errors and processing omissions. Without adequate controls, the losses can be significant, more than most people can imagine. I will give examples in a later chapter of how costly the absence of IT controls or just having minimal controls can be.

➢ Adequate control design and effective execution are now mandated by federal legislature, and failure to comply will result in significant penalties being imposed. Executive management now has an increased legal liability. The mandate by the federal government is not new, but Sarbanes Oxley legislature has given it a mouthful of teeth.

➢ The Foreign Corrupt Practices Act of 1977, that preceded Sarbanes Oxley legislature, changed the Securities and Exchange Act of 1934 to address the authorization and recording of transactions.

➢ As a result of the tremendous costs and time involved in developing complex systems, top management is looking more closely at internal control functions.

➢ Computer crime is becoming a major source of risk in many corporations. How many of the corporate scandals of recent years might have been detected, if not prevented, if basic controls had been in place? How many of the Enron, Worldcom, Xerox scandals would have occurred if there had been adequate controls? Not an easy question to answer, but certainly one which should be asked.

➢ As business organizations convert their old systems to more modern systems and data bases, the failure of the conversion, without adequate control, can be catastrophic to the corporation. Conversion must be successful, and planning is critical up front to ensure that controls are in place, with checks and balances along every step of the conversion process.

➢ Controls are needed to prevent breach of privacy and to protect corporations' confidential or proprietary information. With hackers more numerous, better educated, smarter, more dangerous, and more brazen than ever before, protection via security controls is not a luxury that only very profitable corporations can afford. Hacking is a game to some, a challenge to others, but destructive and unaffordable to most corporations. Even if confidential and proprietary information are not breached, disruption to the company's operation by hackers breaking into systems can be catastrophic.

Control Benefits

The following are benefits that you can realize from the installation of adequate IT controls. They can:

➢ **Position you to comply with federal legislature**. This is especially true with regard to Sarbanes Oxley and should help keep you from being subjected to penalties and /or heavy fines.

- ➢ **Help you pass any audit.** It is no guarantee that you will pass an audit with adequate IT controls, but you certainly will improve your chances.
- ➢ **Provide early warning of processing problems.** The earlier the detection of processing errors, the lower the cost of correction. The cost of fixing errors rises exponentially with the passing of time. You want to identify problems as soon as possible, and with the right detective controls in place, you should succeed.
- ➢ **Deter fraudulent activity.** Again, there is no guarantee, but the installation of adequate controls is definitely a potential deterrent.
- ➢ **Reduce maintenance costs.** Adequate controls can prevent application and system failures, resulting in a reduction of costs associated with the maintenance required to ensure that applications are up and running.
- ➢ **Reduce maintenance headcount/increase development headcount available for next project.** If there are fewer resources assigned to maintaining applications because of adequate controls and application stability, you can reassign these resources to new projects.
- ➢ **Reduce cost associated with administrative corrective action.** If application errors increase because of control weaknesses, you will likely be spending more money on the administrative actions required for corrective action.
- ➢ **Provide assistance in evaluating IT performance and processing efficiency.** Yes, controls can be implemented that will help you evaluate performance.
- ➢ **Provide measurements to evaluate end user satisfaction.** Throughput, timeliness, and accuracy measurements can be of significant help to you and your customers.
- ➢ **Provide recoverability in case of disaster.** Hurricanes, tornadoes, floods, power outages, terrorism and other disasters can bring your operations to a halt without recovery controls.
- ➢ **Reduce operational costs.** The better controlled your applications and systems, the less expensive it will be to keep them operational.
- ➢ **Improve completeness, timeliness and quality of processing.** Having adequate controls can play a major role in achieving these objectives.
- ➢ **Establish accountability.** The right controls assist in assigning accountability.
- ➢ **Provide auditability.** If controls are implemented effectively at the right process steps, then you will have audit trails generated that will demonstrate auditability.

Control Axioms

The following are control axioms that should be helpful:

> **The primary responsibility for overall control resides with top management**. Sarbanes Oxley assigns accountability at the highest level and that is where it should be. Top executives can no longer plead ignorance and take the position that they were not aware of the actions of their management teams. The former Worldcom CEO, Bernard Ebbers, has been convicted and sentenced to jail even though he pleaded ignorance at his trial, claiming that he was not aware that some of the key financial documents showed glaring accounting irregularities.

> **Application controls must be reviewed before and after installation**. Controls need to be independently reviewed before implementation, and during design and development. However, even with well-designed controls, you can have weak execution. Reviewing controls after a new application or system is operational for a measurable period of time is extremely beneficial.

> **Management must set objectives and assign accountability for effective implementation of adequate controls.** The only way that an infrastructure within a corporation can effectively achieve a sound audit control posture is if there is full support and endorsement from the CEO, CFO, CIO, and other executives. Your management teams cannot be effective in enforcing controls if the CEO is not behind them 100%. Top management needs to set objectives and put an infrastructure in place for the effective implementation of controls. For successful results, actions of the senior management team will need to be monitored, and they must be held accountable.

> **Controls must be auditable**. If you cannot demonstrate the design and execution of your controls with adequate documentation you will be in jeopardy of failing an audit. I have conducted numerous audits where I was told that controls were in place—there was no audit trail to provide evidence. Auditors are extremely skeptical and need to be shown; they want proof.

> **Controls must be jointly developed by users/owners and IT personnel**. Controls need to be developed by everyone who is in the game and who has a role. They should not be established without taking all users into consideration. For example, if you are an application development manager designing controls for application recovery, you should design these controls with operational personnel who will probably be relying on well-documented run books with instructions

for keeping applications and systems running. You should also consult application owners and end users who understand business needs regarding the availability of critical applications and can help in establishing recovery requirements and acceptable application down time parameters. When designing controls, consulting other organizations you interface with is a positive step and should be strongly considered.

➢ **Application controls are not to be compromised in order to meet schedules.** Corners should not be cut. You will pay for it in the long run. When I was designing new applications, we were under tight schedules. Unfortunately, in my first major application, we did not focus on controls the way we should have and focused more on meeting the deadline. We met the deadline-but I spent more then a year putting out fires and keeping the application running after it was installed. Because of control issues, the application frequently aborted and I was called in to resolve problems at all hours. Living with my own creation was a very valuable lesson. The next application that I designed was better controlled and I slept at night. There is merit to assigning programmers to the development of new applications only after they have experience in maintaining existing applications. There is valuable knowledge that could be obtained and errors that could be avoided when they become involved in application development.

➢ **It will be exponentially more expensive to retrofit controls into projects after they have been designed and operational.** I have experienced this only too well. In the scenario above where we compromised on controls to meet schedules, it was much more expensive to retrofit the controls into the systems after we went live then if we had designed them up front. It is analogous to building a new house: it's a lot cheaper to put a solar heating system into a house when it is being built than after construction is completed. To use an old adage, "Pay me now or pay me later."

Principles of Control

Following are a list of control principles that are described and referred to at greater lengths within subsequent sections of this book. This is just an overview to, I hope, help drive these points home.

➢ **Separate responsibilities.**
The most effective, basic control that every auditor searches for is segregation of duties, also referred to as separation of duties. Both

terms refer to the establishment of separate roles and responsibilities. If adequate separation of duties exists, you will probably need to have collusion between multiple parties to circumvent controls and commit an intentional act or even unintentional act that will result in processing weaknesses or unauthorized access. Separation of duties must prevail in designing, programming, testing, and installing of controls and auditability features, as well as in the operational environment.

> **Ensure that control processes have procedures, and that procedures are executed in a timely manner.**

All processes that involve activities that need to be controlled, need to have documented control procedures that indicate how, where, and who will exercise the control activity. Okay, you have controls and procedures in place. Is that all that you need to have a well controlled operation and pass an audit? Absolutely not, you must validate that these control activities have been executed in a timely fashion. Procedures without execution, negate control. Sarbanes Oxley legislature dictates that outside auditors must "attest" to the effectiveness of control implementation. Your internal auditing organization should review and validate the effective and timely execution of controls before any outside auditor arrives at the scene.

> **Use manual controls where automation is not possible.**

Manual controls are more prone to human error. There is no doubt that automated controls are more effective. However, manual controls/ procedures are an integral part of any controls review and should not be overlooked. They should be used where it is not possible to use automated controls and, needless to say, are better than not having any controls. For manual controls to be effective they will usually require checks and balances, and they are costly. But if, due to technology issues, automated controls are not possible or feasible, ensure that there are adequate checks and balances on the manual control activities. In some cases you will be combining automated and manual controls. For example, you might have a system-generated report that indicates everyone who has access to your Accounts Payables system, but you might need a manual review to validate their business needs and to initiate action to remove unwarranted access.

> **Conduct annual control reviews to see that the controls are still valid and that they are executing effectively.**

As business processes, environments, and personnel change, documented control procedures will most likely have to change as well. Not only should control procedures and control points be reviewed annually to see if they are still valid and if the documentation needs to be updated, but control activities should be executed annually to see if they are still effective.

> **Mitigate business risks wherever possible by establishing controls.**

Businesses risks need to be frequently re-evaluated to determine their severity. If there is greater business risk due to control weaknesses being identified then a new control procedure might have to established, or an existing control procedure enhanced, to mitigate the risk.

> **Document controls and control points.**

Once processes are documented, it is essential to identify and document where controls need to be established (control points) and then to document the control procedures corresponding to each control point. It is a futile exercise to try to establish controls without reviewing documented processes to determine where exposures might lie without adequate controls.

> **Keep controls simple**

If you design overly-complex, difficult to execute control procedures, they may lose their effectiveness. Keep controls effective but as simple as possible.

> **Localize and reduce exposures**

Establish as many control points as needed, as close to each other as possible to ensure maximum control with the fewest exposures. Be careful not to over control, (see below), but be sure that all exposures are addressed.

> **Consider cost effectiveness**

It is critical to realize that the cost of adding controls is often more than justified by the savings. Many times I have heard managers say that their corporations could not afford the expense of adding all of the controls recommended by auditors. Controls are now mandated by the federal government and you probably will not be able to afford the luxury of not complying with control requirements. Nor can you afford not to design and establish IT controls, because failure to do so will probably cost you more in the long run. Recovering from control problems and retroactively establishing controls after applications and processes are operational could result in significant costs. You will be faced with complex decisions, weighing costs of adding control versus the benefits of a more established control environment. You will need to do what is right for your organization, and balance controls with business needs. Neither the establishment of controls, nor the execution of control procedures, is an exact science, and they are riddled with challenges that will put you to the test. You need to ensure that you are audit ready and in compliance with federal regulations (e.g., Sarbanes

Oxley legislature) but you need to design controls that are cost effective. If the cost of implementing and executing the control is more than the business loss associated with the exposure, then reevaluate and redesign. Remember to maintain a *common cent$* approach to controls. Controls are needed, are essential, and should not be avoided—but remember to always design and implement controls that are not only effective but *cost* effective. There are many ways to implement effective control activities; use good judgment and explore all possibilities.

Federal Regulations Controls

Business Needs   Common Sense

> **Don't over control**
  As indicated above, you want to establish as many control points as needed to effectively address and reduce potential exposures. But don't over control. If one control will suffice instead of two, use one. This is a judgment call, but an important exercise, as over controlling could be detrimental to your processes executing in a timely fashion. Over controlling could bring your business to its knees. You will then have a very well controlled environment but business functions could take much longer to execute than you can afford.

> **Conduct Risk Assessments**
  Risk assessments play a significant role at two crucial stages. First, controls should be initially established where the business risk is greatest. After effective design and implementation of controls, other areas of vulnerability can be explored and controls established where business risk is lower and controls are still warranted. Second, your internal audit organization may not have the resources and time to conduct internal reviews on all of your IT controls. The internal audit organization should conduct a business risk analysis and prioritize their audits based on critical business areas, likelihood of occurrence,

business impact, and loss of revenue due to control exposures. Get the biggest bang for your dollar.

Summary

Every corporate executive must understand the importance and benefits of controls. They must be educated to realize that they can't take controls for granted, and to know when they need to establish controls or enhance their existing controls. They need to be able to identify their weaknesses as well as to understand the business rationale of establishing controls. They will need to weigh the costs of implementing controls and the benefits to be derived. They will need to understand how to implement controls that are both successful in reducing or eliminating exposures, and the most economical, cost effective controls for the company.

They need to appreciate the axiom, "pay now or pay later," with regard to controls. They must be audit ready and not have an illusion of control that could lead to disastrous consequences, both from a business loss and an audit perspective. They need to see to it that controls are designed wherever needed. They need to validate the existence of procedures to apply to those controls and they need to verify that the procedures are being effectively executed, ensuring compliance. Support needs to stem from the CEO, where accountability lies, and responsibility needs to permeate throughout the organization with management held responsible for effective implementation. A daunting task to undertake, but one that cannot be avoided. There is too much at risk.

Chapter Four

Control Definitions

"In modern business it is not the crook who is to be feared most, it is the honest man who doesn't know what he is doing."

—William Wordsworth

Introduction

IT controls, effectively installed, should be a deterrent and detector of criminal activity and fraudulent behavior. However, William Wordsworth's words, "In modern business it is not the crook who is to be feared most, it is the honest man who doesn't know what he is doing," are as true today as they were in his time. Most numerous IT errors in processing are caused not by crooks but by honest employees in unintentional, careless error. These employees are basically trustworthy and well-intentioned, but need to be better educated to design, establish, and execute various types of controls that will reduce and/or detect erroneous processing. Imagine yourself in the following situation:

Let us assume that your department is responsible for the production scheduling, staging, running and balancing of billing applications for the corporation. One night, after five hours of running the Purchase Billing Application, your administrator is balancing the run. He has verified all input, output and processing totals. However, in recording the totals for the run, he notices that they are similar to the Purchase Billing totals from the previous month. Upon closer examination, he realizes that they are more then similar; they are identical. He is aware that there is a problem and a red flag is raised. He calls the individual in the external organization responsible for transmitting the tape and informs him that a duplicate tape was sent.

Fortunately, the erroneous processing was spotted by your administrator before the accounts receivables run and before erroneous ledger entries were made. What we have here is what is commonly referred to as a "detective control". The question that should come to mind is, "Could this have been prevented early in the process with a "preventive control?" The detective control was valuable and saved extensive downstream problems, but you probably could have saved the five hours of erroneous billing application processing.

You decide to get your department together and ask them to suggest a preventive control, an edit at the start of the billing cycle that would have stopped the erroneous duplicate tape from being processed. They call the programming department and after a brief round table discussion, the suggestion is made to add a creation date to the header record that currently exists, with dollar and record counts used for balancing. This creation date is stored in a table for each run in the previous 12-month period. Before the billing application runs there can be an edit of the creation date that can be matched to the last creation date that has been stored in a table. If they match, the run is stopped before further processing of the duplicate transmission. More than five hours will have been saved plus the time the administrator would have spent on detecting the problem and addressing it. This control that stops duplicate processing up front is referred to as a "preventive control".

This is a simplified example but illustrates the value of having a preventive control in place, if possible, and not relying solely on a detective control. Applications, when they are designed, should have both.

In this chapter, in addition to different control types (e.g., preventive, detective and corrective) I will also be describing what is generally regarded as the single most effective control that should be in place, "Separation of Duties".

Control Types

There are numerous control types to be familiar with: preventive controls, deterrent controls, detective controls, reporting controls, corrective controls and recovery controls. These controls can be either manual or automated.

➢ ***Preventive Controls***—Companies should maintain internal controls that provide reasonable assurance that fraudulent or erroneous reporting can be prevented or subject to early detection. Preventive controls mitigate or stop an event from occurring. They are designed at the point of entry.

Preventive controls are usually passive. They are not 100% effective. When breached they lose their effectiveness and need to be backed up by additional controls, usually detective controls.

Examples of preventive controls are:

- Passwords that stop unauthorized access to systems
- Badge readers that are required to gain access to buildings
- Edits and rejections of erroneous data before it is entered into computer applications (e.g. the duplicate transmission above)
- Assurance that sensitive records requiring approvals before being processed are actually approved (e.g. accounts payable of a specified dollar amount)
- Door locks

➤ **_Deterrent controls_**—Deterrent controls discourage or restrain one from acting or proceeding through fear or doubt. They can also restrain or hinder an event.

Examples of deterrent controls are:

- The knowledge that systems are password protected
- Security guards sitting at entrances to buildings
- A sign on a window of a car warning of an alarm system
- The existence of an independent audit committee

➤ **_Detective controls_**—Detective controls reveal or discover unwanted events and offer evidence of trespass. Detective controls find errors for later correction. They are generally the least costly. They often necessitate rework or investigation after the error has been identified. They are usually very effective.

Examples of detective controls are:

- Overdrafts
- Out of balance records/accounts
- After hours security checks
- Unsubstantiated accounting entries
- Absence of documented authorizations when required
- Various types of alarms (e.g. smoke, fire)
- Data base reconciliations

➢ **Reporting controls**—Reporting controls document an event, a situation, or a trespass. Upon detection of an unwarranted event, it is essential that some sort of report be generated.

Examples of reporting controls are:

- Reports being generated for out-of-balance records or unreconciled accounts
- A process to report violations or suspicious activity to executive management. An example would be a list of unauthorized access to the payroll system
- Written audit reports where exposures are documented

➢ **Corrective controls**—Corrective controls remedy or set right an unwanted event. These controls detect errors and attempt to correct them immediately.

Examples of corrective controls are:

- The automated or manual correction of rejected computer processing
- The submission of omitted records
- The enforcement of disciplinary action against personnel engaged in fraudulent activities

> **Recovery controls**—Recovery controls regain or make good the effect of an unwanted event. This type of control is used mainly in situations of hardware errors but can be used in the case of software failure.
> Examples of recovery controls are:
>
> - Software automatically recovering and restarting communication circuits when there is a communications failure
> - Automatic restart of application programs in the event of failure
> - Tape or disc rereads

A well controlled IT organization will have most, if not all of these control types implemented and they will reinforce each other. Time should be spent within every IT organization deciding, designing, implementing and executing the types of controls that are best suited for its environment.

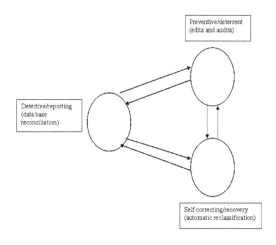

Separation of Duties

The most effective and basic control in any organization is separation of duties (SOD). Separation of duties is the segregation of responsibilities and duties with regard to the various functional components of the organization; SOD is sometimes referred to as segregation of duties. Basically, the same person should not have responsibility for more than one of the following functions within a particular business process:

> - Custody/ access to an asset
> - Performance of asset record keeping
> - Authorization of changes to the asset
> - Verification of the asset or perform independent checks

Separation of duties is the most effective control that can be implemented for the prevention (via segregation of job functions) and detection (via manual checks and balances) of unwanted events. If adequate separation of duties is established it will require collusion, in most situations, for fraudulent activities to take place. Every IT audit will focus on separation of duties and the auditee will need to not only state that separation of duties has been effectively established, but will need to validate and demonstrate effective execution.

One of the most commonly used excuses for not installing adequate separation of duties is a resource issue. There are many companies that believe that they can not afford the expense of hiring additional personnel to provide for separation of duties. However, separation of duties can sometimes, although not always, be accomplished without additional resource. All possibilities should be explored to see which functions can be split, so that the same individual is not performing two or more critical functions resulting in a separation of duties conflict.

When you undergo any audit, especially a Sarbanes Oxley audit, separation of duties is looked upon as one of the most effective preventive controls that can be implemented. SOD is not a guarantee that fraudulent or erroneous processing will not take place, but it is recognized as being one of the more successful controls and it is closely examined by auditors. Inadequate separation of duties can be a show-stopper during a Sarbanes Oxley audit, or with any IT audit for that matter.

Separation of duties is not only extremely important in accounting and financial organizations, but auditors will also be looking at separation of duties in the IT community. Inadequate SOD can negatively affect financial reporting, as has become more apparent during the last few years. This book will be focusing on SOD in the IT arena only. Separation of duties will be summarized here but will be mentioned in other chapters as well.

Separation of Duties Examples

Separation of duties should exist within the operations organization as well as within the application development organization and across activities that transcend both organizations. Some controls that need to be in place that an auditor should review for effectiveness are:

- ➢ Segregating duties between computer operational personnel, applications programmers, system programmers, data base administrators, and support personnel.
- ➢ Prohibiting application programmers from having access to production data, or production libraries, unless granted access by data owners.
- ➢ Reviewing that controls are in place to ensure adequate checks and balances, and a third party review when access is granted.
- ➢ Preventing operational personnel from writing code that will be promoted into a production environment.

> Assuring that a developer programmer does not have privileged access to production data to support a production environment, as does a systems programmer.
> Determining that there are adequate controls to prohibit a systems programmer from writing application code.
> Preventing an operator, application programmer or systems programmer from controlling or granting access to production data. This should be restricted to a data base administrator.

Tables

There is a unique SOD question that pertains to tables that grant access to databases and files. Access to these tables, whether external to applications or internal to applications, needs to be adequately controlled. If applications contain access tables it is imperative that separation of duties be established. There should be controls to ensure that the people granting access are not the same as those requesting access. Additionally, the individual who updates application logic or who controls external tables should not be the same individual who is approving and granting access. Usually request forms are submitted by an end user to the individual who updates the access tables. There should be checks and balances intrinsic to the processes that require that the individual who receives the requests is not the person who updates the access tables, and that the request contains adequate approval. Some questions that the auditor should ask are:

> Is the requester who wants access to database or files the same person who updates the access tables?
> Is there an individual who checks for approvals and is this person different than the person who updates the application or application tables?
> Can development programmers grant themselves access without a third party review?
> Can an individual delete a person's access without the application owner's approval?

Separation of Duties Case Studies

Smaller firms have more of a challenge than larger companies in ensuring adequate separation of duties. In a larger company there are more personnel to distribute and disseminate functions among. In a smaller organization, one person is usually performing functions that one, two or many personnel are assigned to in a larger company; they wear multiple hats. They do not have the luxury of being able to establish the "ideal" separation of duties environment. Executives within these companies need to be aware of the risks involved and need to establish whatever separation of duties they can afford. Where separation of duties is limited, check and balance procedures should be installed where possible to mitigate the risks. If one person needs to be responsible for multiple activities that are in conflict and a risk to the business, then his or her actions should be reviewed by another individual, even a manager if necessary. Before I discuss separation of duties that should be adhered to in both organizations, let me present you with case studies based on audits.

Case Study I (small company)

You are the president of a small company. You have less than 250 people working for you with thirty employees in your IT organization headed up by Bill. Bill and his organization, an operations manager and a development manager support the operational as well as the development and maintenance efforts of your fifty applications. An outside accounting organization is conducting a SOX audit at your company and Bill has informed them that due to limited resources, and budget constraints against hiring additional IT resources, there are separation of duties exposures. Apparently Bill has documented a business risk acceptance and obtained your approval. There are two operational personnel who have DBA responsibility, assign passwords, issue and revoke user ids and monitor application performance as well. These two back each other up. Your development team consists of fifteen developers, some who write new code and some who promote code. You also have developers who perform both functions. You realize that the developers should not be promoting code but they have all the knowledge. There is no one else who can do the job, you need them to perform these tasks to keep applications running, and your customer has no problem with this separation of duties concern. You explain this situation to the auditors; do you think that they will accept it? They probably will not. They will want to know why you can not install checks and balances such as one developer writing the code and another promoting the code. They will want to know why you can't have secondary controls exercised by an independent party that would detect if unauthorized code had been promoted, such as a manager or another developer.

Case Study: II (large corporation)

You are the CIO at a fairly large corporation. Your outside accounting organization has announced that they are starting their SOX audit. They have arrived at the headquarters of your IT organization. Three months ago your IT organization underwent an audit from your internal audit staff that resulted in minor findings, and you feel pretty comfortable. The outside auditors (Stan, Jim, Nancy and Carol) have arrived at the headquarters of your IT organization.

The auditors start their interview process after they have had a kickoff meeting. Stan and Carol want to talk to the application support senior manger and his staff. Stan asks him if any of his developers have access to production data. He tells them that the mainframe developers have read access to production but not update capability unless update access is specifically granted by the owner of the data. Carol wants to know when developers would need to update production data or production libraries. She wants to know the process for granting update access to production libraries/data and how it is controlled.

Your senior manager tells Carol that right now none of the mainframe developers have update access to the production program libraries. There is a librarian in place within the Operations organization, who promotes code and none of the mainframe developers promote code. Your senior manger feels that with two different organizations in place, duties are effectively segregated. He does not realize that he is going to be subjected to further inquiries.

Stan then asks not if any of the developers promote code but "Can they promote code? Are there preventive controls in place to prevent them from accessing the production libraries?" Your senior manager tells Stan and Carol that there are preventive access controls in place. RACF is used to grant access and none of the developers have been granted access. The access is granted by a DBA who is not a developer. The DBA works in the Operations organization. Stan, as most auditors will, wants to verify this. He asks to be shown a list of mainframe developers and what they have access to. He is told that he will have the list by the next day.

The senior manager reacts quickly and asks his development managers for a list of each department's development personnel and their access. He hands this over to Stan and Carol. They are now joined by Jim and Nancy, two additional auditors, who have been assigned to help with the separation of duties audit. Nancy asks how the auditors would know if that list actually represents the access that the developers have. Nancy asks for a "system generated" list. Your senior manager goes back and asks his managers for system generated access lists. Rather than one list being generated for each department, the RACF administrator is asked to help and he generates a single access list for all of the mainframe developers. Your senior manager presents this system generated list to Jim and Nancy the next day.

Jim and Nancy review the list the next day and ask you to identify production data sets. When you do, Nancy asks why some of the developers have update access to certain production libraries. Your senior manager is surprised to see this as he was told by his management staff and lead staff personnel that none of the mainframe developers had update access to production libraries. He is embarrassed now and asks his managers for an explanation. After some research it is discovered that two developers have update access to production libraries because they were at one time database administrators. They changed their career paths but their access was never revoked.

Jim makes some notes and then asks, "How often is access reviewed to validate that people who no longer have a business need to access production libraries have had their access revoked?" Your management team answers that it is suppose to be done annually. Of course Jim asks for verification of the last revalidation. Your management team is able to produce it. It was done eleven months ago. Nancy then asks, "When did the two developers change their careers and transfer to the development organization after being DBAs?" They are told that they transferred seven months ago.

Then Nancy asks you "Do you have a process in place to revoke access when they transfer?" Your senior manager replies that his management is suppose to notify the RACF administrator to revoke access if there is no longer a business need. Jim and Nancy then verify with your senior manager that there was an exposure for seven months when these two developers *could* have migrated their own code to production and he has to agree.

Jim and Nancy leave production program libraries alone and ask about access to production data. It was stated earlier that mainframe developers could have access but if they needed access to production data it would have to be approved by the owner of the production data. There are times when the developers need to read and change production data in case of production emergencies. Nancy asks for the procedure and you show it to her. She then asks if there is any monitoring done when anyone makes a change to production data. Your manager tells them that the owner of the production data has someone on his staff who releases a temporary id to the developer to access production data, reviews the change that was made, initials it and then revokes the temporary access. Your senior manager tells the auditors that developers should never be able to update production data unless authorized and controlled by the owner.

Now Al and Carol ask you about the distributed environment. Your managers tell them that they have small staffs and that developers promote their own code. RACF does not play a role for the UNIX and Windows environments that they support and they do not have the resources to separate responsibilities and ensure separation of duties. The auditors then ask a few questions focusing on checks and balances and on detective controls since there are no system preventive controls in this environment. They ask what secondary or manual controls are in place to "detect" unauthorized access. Your senior manager confidently tells the auditors that one developer is assigned to make coding changes to a specific application and another developer promotes the code. For another application they switch roles. Jim then asks your senior manager if the developer who wrote the code could promote the code and how would that be detected. Your management team is asked if there is any manual monitoring to ensure that all changes that were promoted to production were in fact authorized. Your senior manager does not have an answer and sees Nancy writing notes in her note book. And it goes on and on; the questions keep coming. Most of your management team would opt for root canal rather than be subjected to this audit.

Following is an example of an IT Separation of Duties Matrix. This should give you an overview of where potential exposures exist and an idea of where segregating duties would be advantageous.

IT Separation of Duties Matrix

Separation of Duties Matrix	Request access to production data	Approve access to production data	Provide access to production data	Update production data	Approve request to change code	Approve access to code	Change application code	Approve code promotion to UAT	Promote Code to UAT	Create /Develop UAT Data	Execute UAT	Approve code promotion to production	Promote code to production	Update tables that provide access
1 Request access to production data	▪	N	N	N	Y	Y	Y	Y	Y	Y	Y	N	N	Y
2 Approve access to prod data (owner)	N	▪	N	N	Y	N	N	N	N	N	Y	N	Y	Y
3 Provide access to prod data (DBA)	N	N	▪	N	N	N	N	N	N	N	N	N	Y	Y
4 Update production data (DBA)	N	N	N	▪	N	N	Y	N	Y	Y	Y	N	N	Y
5 Approve request to change code (owner)	Y	Y	N	N	▪	N	N	N	N	Y	Y	Y	N	N
6 Approve access to code (dev mgr)	Y	N	N	N	N	▪	N	Y	N	N	N	N	N	N
7 Change application code (developer)	Y	N	N	Y	N	N	▪	N	Y	Y	Y	N	N	Y
8 Approve UAT code promotion (owner)	Y	Y	N	N	Y	N	N	▪	N	Y	Y	Y	N	N
9 Promote code to UAT (developer)	Y	N	N	Y	N	N	Y	N	▪	Y	Y	N	N	Y
10 Create/develop UAT data (owner rep)	Y	Y	N	Y	N	N	Y	N	Y	▪	Y	N	N	N
11 Execute UAT (owner rep)	Y	N	N	N	Y	N	N	Y	N	Y	▪	Y	N	N
12 Approve prod code promotion (owner)	Y	Y	N	N	Y	N	N	Y	N	Y	Y	▪	N	Y
13 Promote code/tables to production (operations)	N	N	N	N	N	N	N	N	N	N	N	N	▪	N
14 Update ext tables that provide prod access (owner rep)	Y	N	N	N	N	N	N	Y	N	Y	Y	N	N	▪

Creating and implementing an SOD matrix is not an exact science and there will be different responsibilities assigned depending on your company's size, available resources and organizational roles. For example, the creation/ development and execution of Uses Acceptance testing (UAT) can be performed by developers or owner organizations. Let's look a little closer.

Some notes on the matrix:

Request Access to Production Data—This is the individual who requests read or update access to production data; it can be a developer, database administrator or end user. This individual should not approve access or provide access to production data.

Approve Access to Production Data—This individual is the owner of the data, or his or her delegate, who reviews the business reason for data access and approves access. This should not be the person who requests or provides access to production data nor should it be someone who can update production data.

Provide Access to Production Data—This individual is usually someone in operations, a database administrator, who grants access to individuals who have been approved. This individual must not be an approver.

Update Production Data—A database administrator is usually approved to update production data as a result of a business need or in their daily job performance. A database administrator usually has pre-approval to update production data by an owner but there needs to an audit trail of their activity. *As a rule, developers should not be able to update production data.* This is sometimes looked upon as a cardinal sin. However, depending upon your organizational structure and resource limitation there might be a need for a developer to update production data and correct it in case of an emergency. If a developer is to update production data, then his or her activity needs to be monitored with an independent reviewer to validate that they were authorized and approved by the owner and that the changes were valid. This detective control, also refereed to a secondary control, requires that the independent reviewer sign off after their review with the documentation maintained as an audit trial. The retention period of this audit trail needs to be established by your CGO.

Approve Request to Change Code—Application code that needs to be updated must be approved by a business application owner or their delegate. The application owner may or may not be the same individual who is the data owner. These roles need to be defined for each organization.

Approve Access to Code—If an application developer needs to access source code to make a change, then the developer's manager needs to approve their access to the source code library. Approval to access the source code library should not be given to the same individual who grants access. You do not want an individual approving their own access. The developer's manager should not be allowed to change application code unless access to the source code library is granted by another manager.

Change Application Code—Only an application developer should be allowed to change application code. The only exception would be an application manager, as indicated above.

Approve Code Promotion to UAT—Migrating code to a library where user acceptance testing (UAT) is performed should be approved by the business application owner or their delegate.

Promote Code to UAT—An application developer promotes code to the UAT library.

Create/Develop UAT Data—In some organizations the developers create UAT data and in some organizations the business application owner or their delegate creates UAT data.

Execute UAT—The execution of UAT can be done by the individual who created the test data or by someone else. However, this individual should not be the person who changed the application code. Separation of duties should be evident in this case.

Approve Code Promotion to Production—This can only be done by the business application owner or their delegate. A developer or the developer's management can never provide this approval. Approval should be obtained prior to moving the code to production. If there is an emergency and the owner's documented approval cannot be obtained, then there needs to be post approval for audit purposes.

Promote Code to Production—Migration of code to the production library should be done by a librarian, usually someone in operations, but certainly by an individual who is not an application developer responsible for coding. In some organizations and environments, it might not be possible to have a librarian or separate individual perform the promotion and the developer might have to perform that function. *If the developer can update production libraries, then there is not adequate separation of duties, and secondary controls, as discussed above, need to be put in place and effectively executed.* If the developer needs permanent access, then that access needs to be approved by the owner and all production update activity needs to be independently monitored to ensure that all updates were authorized. The independent reviewer needs to sign off on the review and the documentation that was reviewed retained. If temporary access is needed, a temporary ID and password can be granted when code needs to be promoted and removed afterwards. The developer's update activity must also be monitored with an audit trail maintained.

Update tables that provide access to production databases or production data—If tables are internal to applications, then the controls over table updates and the separation of duties controls are the same as code changes where the change needs to be audited and separation of duties or secondary controls needs to be in place for promotion. If the tables that grant access are external tables, then the person who updates the tables is usually an administrator or end user and this individual should not have the capability to grant access or to update production. This individual also needs to have owner approval to update the access tables.

I will be discussing separation of duties in other chapters as well; it is a major control and one of the most effective that can be established. It is important to remember that the matrix above is just an example of how roles can be segregated and is not meant to be all-inclusive. A Separation of duties matrix is tailored for the unique business need of each organization.

Summary

It is important that every corporate manager understands what different control types are so that they can make an educated decision on the controls they should establish.

Controls are put in place to prevent or detect not only fraudulent activity but also unintentional erroneous processing. Most of the control deficiencies in IT processing are not a result of intentional errors but are a result of a lack of education or compliance by honest people. If preventive controls can not be put in place then detective controls should be installed. The best scenario is to have both preventive and detective controls established.

The most effective control is the establishment of adequate separation of duties where roles and responsibilities are segregated. Adequate secondary controls need to be in place where separation of duties is not possible or feasible.

The CGO and CEO should sit down and ask senior management to complete the following questionnaire. The completion of this questionnaire should be followed by internal audit staffs validating the responses to these questions.

1. Are preventive controls designed within your IT organization?
2. Are they being executed effectively?
3. Are detective controls designed within you organization?
4. Are they being executed effectively?
5. Has your management team received education on the types of controls and separation of duties?
6. Do you have a separation of duties matrix in place for your organization?
7. Are separation of duties controls established and effectively executed to enforce your separation of duties matrix?

8. Are there separation of duties where developers can not promote code to production libraries?
9. In the case where developers update production libraries, is there a process is place for secondary controls to independently monitor production updates?
10. Is there a list of application owners who can approve production updates?
11. Is there a separate list of production data owners if this list is not the same as the list of application owners?
12. Are operational personnel restricted from writing code that will be promoted to production?

Chapter Five

Establishment of a Sound IT Control Infrastructure

"The beginning is the most important part of the work."

—Plato

Introduction

I have discussed the importance and benefits of controls, the establishment of processes and procedures and the necessity of ensuring effective execution. Where does it start? How can an infrastructure be put in to place to achieve all this and whose responsibility is it? I mentioned in the previous chapter that Sarbanes Oxley holds the CEO responsible for the certification of effective controls. However, a CEO is not totally independent, and as we have seen in recent corporate scandals, CEOs have been indicted as a result of misappropriation of funds or being responsible for the falsification of financial statements and unethical behavior. The ultimate responsibility lies with the board of directors, and a select group of board members called the audit committee. It is this committee whose job it is to protect the shareholders and stockholders. Independence is key and there needs to be an independent audit organization and executive. If Sarbanes Oxley is holding the CEO responsible then who is monitoring his or her actions? Where is the company's governance committee and who do they report to?

In this chapter I discuss and inject my personal opinion as to the roles, responsibilities and makeup of the board of directors, the audit committee, the chief governance officer (CGO) and the audit teams. I use the term CGO but many corporations today have a chief auditing executive (CAE) who fulfills many, if not all, of the same functions. Whenever I use the term CGO it can be interchanged with CAE. I will be talking about a new concept and a change in an existing paradigm, the reporting of the CGO directly to the audit committee and not to the CEO as is true with many corporations today. If the CGO were to report to the CEO, the lack of independence would present a potential conflict of interest as well as raise ethical and loyalty questions.

You might believe that the CGO can still report to the CEO and that the watchdog of the CEO's actions is the external audit firm who needs to 'attest' to the effective execution of controls and control irregularities. The problem with this train of thought is that the external audit review is too late. If there are irregularities in financial reporting, inappropriate bookkeeping, or just total control breakdown, then these situations should be discovered by an independent internal audit organization *before* an external audit.

The internal audit infrastructure is the beginning. And as Plato said, the beginning is the most important part of the work. It is the building block from which corporate governance and Sarbanes Oxley compliance can be achieved. The reporting hierarchy may be new, but the establishment of the right infrastructure, one that will stand up to the scrutiny of outside auditors and/or federal regulators, one that will ensure integrity and get the job done is crucial to success.

Board of Directors

Unfortunately many corporations today, which have established internal auditing organizations, have not established true independence. Internal auditors report to a CEO or CFO and the result is the proverbial "fox in the hen house". We need to remove the internal audit organization from the control and direction setting of the CEO and/or CFO, accountable for corporate profits, and establish a direct reporting line to the board of directors.

The likelihood of establishing an *effective* audit readiness infrastructure relies on a commitment by the board of directors to fully support such an effort. Without their support and backing, the effectiveness of an internal audit infrastructure will be limited. The board of directors needs to endorse the establishment of an *independent* organization reporting directly to them. The adoption of this new approach is essential for success.

Responsibilities of the board of directors should include:

➤ **The selection of an audit committee.** The board of directors should select an audit committee from its membership. The audit committee should be comprised of board members who are thoroughly independent. The Sarbanes-Oxley Act of 2002, which is a major step towards cracking down on corporate fraud, requires more independence among board members. It requires that audit committee members be on the company's board, but independent: they can not be current officers of the company or its subsidiaries. Independence means that they are free from any relationship that, in the opinion of the board, could influence or taint their objectiveness. To be completely independent, members of the audit committee *must not own company stock.* Audit committee members should be paid a straight salary and must not be given stocks or stock options. This could be a disturbing concept for corporate America today, but critical, if we truly desire independence in governance. If you review corporate financial statements today, you will see that in almost every situation, board of director members hold a significant number of shares of company stock. This is acceptable for the CEO, who is accountable for the financial success of the corporation. However, it is not acceptable for audit committee members, who are accountable for the accuracy and integrity of financial reporting and who must be void of any conflicting interests that might jeopardize their objectiveness. Stock and stock option owners are primarily interested in the stock price above everything else, which could result in a conflict of interest when controls and ethical behavior enter the picture. Stock options are risk free instruments that could create conflicts of interest and should not be given to the audit committee.

➢ **Establishing a Charter for the Audit Committee.** The board of directors should establish a charter for the audit committee that addresses the committee's duties and responsibilities. The charter should identify the purpose, authority and responsibilities of the internal audit department including the chief governance officer. The charter should also clearly state an auditor's right to access all records, policies, processes and procedures and to question all personnel about matters under review. The charter should address audit independence and support from the board of directors. The tone set by the board of directors is the most important factor in determining the success of the audit readiness program and in ensuring adequate controls and integrity of financial reporting. They will also need to review the charter annually and modify it, when required.

➢ **Rotation of Audit Committee Members**—The board of directors, who are elected for three-year terms and ratified every year, should limit the assignment of audit committee members that they select to two-year terms. Committee members should be replaced by other "independent" board of director members after their terms expire. Audit committee members serving more than two years can become too comfortable and establish close relationships, which might knowingly or unknowingly result in compromising their independence and objectivity. The effective execution of audit committee responsibilities will frequently determine the survival of the company and their objectivity should never be in doubt.

➢ **Ensuring cooperation**—The board of directors must ensure that the CEO and CFO and their organizations are fully supportive of the efforts of the audit committee and cooperate with any internal audit within their company.

The Audit Committee

The audit committee validates the accuracy of financial reporting. They are a subset of board of directors members, chosen by the entire board, whose daunting task is to regain credibility and confidence of shareholders by fulfilling the awesome responsibilities below.

Responsibilities of the audit committee are:

➢ **Accountability for the accuracy of financial reporting.** The responsibility for the integrity of financial and accounting reports should reside with the CEO, CFO and the accounting organization. However, the ultimate accountability to the shareholders and to the public must reside with the audit committee. The existence of an audit committee is not enough; an audit committee must be vigilant and informed of the control exposures within the company and be ultimately accountable for financial reporting. To be effective, the audit committee and board of director members must have basic accounting knowledge. It is unfortunate today that many board of director members are not educated in basic accounting and can not read a financial statement. It is important that every board of director member who is selected to be on the audit committee have a fundamental accounting background and education so that they can oversee the accuracy of corporate financial statements. This goes beyond Sarbanes-Oxley (section 407) where companies are required to have at least **one** member of their audit committee who is a financial expert.

> **Appointment of a chief governance officer, CGO, or chief accounting executive (CAE) to oversee the audit infrastructure.** The audit committee needs to appoint a chief governance officer or chief accounting executive who will be responsible for the establishment of the audit readiness infrastructure and the development and implementation of an audit readiness program. The audit committee should not only select the CGO or CAE but periodically reevaluate the CGO's or CAE's effectiveness and decide if he or she should be replaced.

> **Review/endorse the Audit Readiness Program.** The audit committee members must be in complete agreement with and endorse an audit readiness program established by the CGO. They must fully support the CGO once the audit readiness program is finalized.

> **Provide Direction.** The audit committee should provide direction to the CGO and recommend changes to the audit readiness program when they feel that it is in the best interests of the company and its shareholders. The audit committee can also authorize special investigations, outside of regularly scheduled audits, when deemed necessary.

> **Establish a written code of business conduct.** A strong ethical code of conduct and acceptable behavior is essential to the well being and continued existence of the company, as well as to the company being able to successfully stand up to public scrutiny. The development of the code will take time but the company must establish the code to fit its environment. It is important to realize that the tightest controls and checks and balances will not always be able to prevent unethical behavior.

It is incumbent on the audit committee to establish and ensure that a code of company ethics is distributed to every company employee, read and understood and adhered to. The committee should review the business conduct code annually as well as monitor compliance.

A code of ethics should include:

a. The need to protect confidential and proprietary information
b. Avoidance of actions resulting in a conflict-of-interest
c. Compliance with federal and state regulatory laws
d. Prohibition of personal use of company equipment and assets
e. Statements that non compliance to the company's code of conduct can result in disciplinary action

➢ **Review audit reports**. The audit committee has a responsibility to review all audit reports and recommendations to all issues, as they deem appropriate.

➢ **Evaluate risks associated with exposures**. The audit committee should evaluate all risks analysis conducted by the CGO and internal auditors for all significant exposures. The committee needs to quantify the potential risk to the company and decide if the cost of corrective action is warranted.

➢ **Ensure that corrective actions are taken to address control weaknesses**. If corrective actions are recommended by the internal auditors and agreed to by the audit committee, then the audit committee must validate that the appropriate management has taken the corrective actions. They must fully support the recommendations of the auditors and the CGO and ensure that the CEO, CFO and their respective management teams implement the corrective actions as dictated. Exposures need closure.

➢ **Review effectiveness of external auditors and recommend rotation of external audit partners**. In addition to overseeing the activity of the *internal audit organization*, the audit committee needs to evaluate the effectiveness and integrity of the *external audit organization*. As a result of their evaluation, they should recommend that either external auditors continue to serve in their role as external auditors for another year, or that they be replaced.

➢ **Recommend rotation of external audit partners**. To minimize the potential of external audit organizations becoming too intertwined and part of the corporate family, reducing their objectivity, the audit committee should insist that the length of service for external audit partners be limited. The audit committee along with the CGO should ensure that external auditor partners be rotated at least every three years to prevent them from becoming too comfortable and relaxed and to avoid potential conflict of interest situations. Let us learn from the

Enron scandal where Arthur Anderson's effectiveness as a watchdog was non-existent. Arthur Anderson, Enron's external auditor, was fined and convicted of shredding Enron documents in the midst of an Enron investigation by the Securities and Exchange Commission. Another incident of external auditors becoming too comfortable occurred on January 30, 2003 when the Securities and Exchange Commission filed a civil fraud complaint against Xerox's external auditors. Senior auditing partners were accused of repeatedly deciding to signoff on bad accounting at Xerox. Stephen M Cutler, the Commission's enforcement director stated that auditors have a critical responsibility in the financial reporting process and that the external auditors and their partners abdicated that responsibility.

➢ **Restrict service of external audit organizations.** Not only should the length of service of external audit partners be limited, but the external audit organization's service should be restricted to ten years at the maximum, provided their annual evaluations are satisfactory. It should be mandated that external audit organizations be replaced after a decade of service to ensure independence.

➢ **Ensure compliance with federal law.** The audit committee is accountable for the company's compliance to the Security and Exchange Committee's rules and Federal laws.

The CGO

The internal audit organization should be headed by a chief governance officer (CGO) who will be appointed by and report directly to the audit committee. The CGO will select a managerial staff that will ensure the establishment of qualified independent audit internal teams. Since the audit teams will also audit the CEO's and other executive's activities, their reviews must be truly independent. They must be given a free hand to operate across the entire corporation, across all business units, organizations and departments, reporting their results directly to the audit committee. The effectiveness of the company's internal audit function depends to a large extent on the objectivity of the audit staff. The internal auditors must be free to perform their audits without interference, anywhere within the corporation. The CEO, although subject to audits of his or her own activity, must instruct management to be fully cooperative with the efforts of any independent internal audit. Opposition to independent reviews may indicate that there is something to hide.

Once there is agreement by the audit committee to the creation of an independent infrastructure, the next step is the selection of a CGO. The first requirement, and the most critical that must be satisfied, is that the credibility of the CGO must be beyond reproach. Candidates for this position must have an unblemished record. They need to be revered in the corporate world as someone who posses a level of integrity, surpassed by none. The highest moral fiber must be intrinsic in their character. Their backgrounds and previous experiences need to be closely scrutinized to ensure that is no doubt concerning their ethics. They will need to be able to demonstrate a loyalty and allegiance to their stockholders and a commitment to uphold the basic ethical beliefs and policies that are declared by the board of directors. It is incumbent on the audit committee to first clearly state their ethical policies and expectations required in fulfilling the position and then choose a CGO whom will best satisfy their requirements.

Other requirements that need to be met by the CGO are to have had a successful background in auditing and to have held executive management positions in this field. Former CEOs, CIOs or CFOs as well as current and previous partners in auditing firms could be candidates and included in this search. The CGO must be a successful executive manager, possess knowledge of corporate finance and business operations and understand the significance of the role of Information Technology in today's corporate America. Since the CGO will report to the audit committee and will be reviewing the activities of CEOs, CFOs, CIOs and other executives, he or she needs to receive a salary that will be compatible with the salaries of top executive officers in the company. To minimize the importance of this job would be shortsighted. The integrity of corporation books is vital to the success and continued operation of most companies, and the executive responsible for ensuring accuracy of financial reporting and business controls needs to be justly compensated.

Responsibilities of the CGO are:

> **Selection of management teams to manage internal audits and to decide scope.** It is essential that the CGO choose qualified management to implement the audit readiness program. The management team is the backbone of the audit infrastructure. These individuals should be employees from within the company who have the same level of integrity as the CGO, at least ten years of experience with the company and successful management experience.

> **Establish the Audit Readiness Program.** The CGO needs to sit with their management team and establish an audit readiness program that will be unanimously approved. The program will only be successful if the audit committee gives the program their full vote of confidence and endorsement. The audit readiness program that is established should focus on "Pro-active Activities" as well as the "Audit Process", both of which are discussed in later chapters.

> **Provide Direction.** The CGO must provide direction to his or her management staff and review audit scopes. For example, the CGO should define external partnerships and ensure that external processes, with regard to partnerships, are clearly documented and adhered to.

> **Develop a process for the written code of business conduct.** The CGO must document a process that will ensure that the written code of business conduct, established by the audit committee is distributed, understood and complied with by all management and personnel in the company. A written code of corporate conduct is essential to establishing an ethical climate for all employees.

> **Review audit reports.** The CGO needs to review all audit reports with the executives who are being audited and impacted to ensure agreement on audit results, recommendations and those items needing corrective actions. In addition, semi—annual meetings should be scheduled with the audit committee to review overall audit readiness and regulatory compliance with emergency meetings convened when necessary. The CEO and CFO should also attend meetings with the audit committee along with corporate counsel and external accountants to ensure compliance with federal laws and SEC regulations. The CGO along with the CEO and CFO should decide on those reports and issues that the audit committee needs to be informed of.

> **Review risks associated with exposures.** The CGO must review the risk assessments documented by the internal audit staffs and recommend whether or not the audit committee should evaluate the risks. Again this decision must be made in agreement with the CEO and CFO.

> **Ensure that corrective actions plans are established to address control weaknesses.** The CGO needs to validate that each exposure is addressed and establish a process to monitor satisfactory execution of corrective action plans until exposures are eliminated.

> **Ensure compliance with federal law.** It is the CGO's responsibility to understand the rules and regulations of all federal regulatory agencies and ensure corporate compliance. The CGO should partner with corporate counsel to satisfy this objective.

> **Coordinate meetings with external auditors.** At least on an annual basis, it is vital that the CGO schedule meetings with the company's external auditors to review and compare audit scopes, and review audit results. This will allow for decisions to be made regarding schedules. It could be detrimental to business continuity if the same organization within the company was subjected to both internal and external audits within a limited time period. These collaborative meetings will also allow each organization to reduce

their audit scope if they feel that another audit organization had effectively reviewed the same business area. It will also allow the CGO and his or her staff to ensure that there is closure to the recommendations made by the external audit organization.

Audit Readiness Program

The audit readiness program as I mentioned above, needs to be designed by the CGO and approved by the audit committee. The value-add of the audit infrastructure is just not in conducting internal audits. The real value of an internal audit infrastructure extends into proactive activities that the CGO and audit teams should be engaged in, described in the audit readiness program. These activities would include defining types of controls, techniques used to identify control weaknesses, and addressing control and ethics education, as well as defining roles and responsibilities for pro-active activities.

Furthermore, the audit readiness program needs to recommend audits to be conducted for the following year, describing in detail the audit process from announcing the audit through distribution of the final audit report. It should also address the process by which all issues will be tracked and reported, whether they have been identified as the result of pro-active activities or audits.

The audit readiness program needs to be revisited each year with regard to the audits that are scoped. As the environment changes, so will the audits that are selected for review. Selected areas or processes to be audited are areas where the risks are the greatest and this could change year to year. For example, if suppliers are playing more and more of a critical role as the business grows, than perhaps the procurement process along with competitive bidding needs to be audited. If executives are traveling more and more, then it might make sense that executive expenses be audited. If financial reporting practices are changing, then maybe the accounting processes need to be reviewed. If outstanding delinquencies are increasing exponentially, then perhaps it is time to audit the accounts receivable process. If outsourcing IT functions becomes a more accepted policy then maybe the audit readiness program needs to align itself with this strategic direction. The audit committee can change the audit scope at any time during the year and have internal audit look at those areas that are deemed important as a result of business, economic or environmental changes.

Audit Teams

In my opinion, one of the most important elements for an efficacious audit readiness program is the composition of the audit team. After all, it is the audit team who is responsible for conducting reviews of policies, procedures and controls and identifying exposures. This is an extremely important role, *a critical role,* often not given enough attention. Auditors need to be not only dedicated, educated and experienced with audit techniques, but knowledgeable about company organizations and processes. When I was a new auditor in my company, I had more than ten years experience with the company. Recruiting new auditors with business experience, I believe, is one of the strengths of my firm. I was selected not only because of my Information Technology (I/T) experience and knowledge, but also because of the insight and cognizance of company processes and procedures I acquired throughout my years with the company. IT was my forte, but I knew enough about other areas of the company to be of significant value to the audit teams and audit leaders when I was assigned to work with them.

I was familiar with various company operational procedures when I started to audit. What I knew about accounts payable, billing, receivables, procurement etc. was minimal, but that knowledge, modest as it was in comparison to my knowledge of IT, made me more of a "value add" than if I had been hired without any such experience. Other members of the audit staff had expertise in these processes and because of their many years of business experience, had been introduced to the world of IT. While I was experienced enough to lead them in an IT audit, they knew enough about the fundamentals of IT and how it is integrated in business functions, to be of significant value to me. I can not say enough about the value of business experience with regard to effective auditing.

There are many companies today who recruit new auditors directly from college. Although they may be bright, they frequently lack the experience to be effective internal auditors. They are usually schooled in fundamental sound accounting practices or in IT but they need a lot more. I have seen bright young auditors move through each audit step of their extensive documented checklists as thoroughly as possible, but they fall short when trying to evaluate what the real business impact is to a potential exposure. They just don't have enough business acumen to know if they have uncovered a real exposure or not. They need to answer that eternal audit question, "So what?" What does it matter if a process is not documented or a procedure is not followed? What is the business exposure? What is the business impact of the control deficiency? As an auditee, I have observed outside external audit firms assigning new auditors who have little business experience to audit business processes or IT functions that they were totally unfamiliar with. They have been on the threshold of significant issues without realizing it. On the flip side, I have seen inexperienced auditors make mountains out of molehills and inflate issues out of proportion, wasting not only their time but also the precious time of managers because they were not applying practical experience. For the most part, they are navigating down a checklist that they have been taught to use in a classroom setting. They need to understand the business impact of the issue and the ramifications if the issue is not adequately addressed. This is an essential ingredient in the recipe of a successful auditor. There is too much at stake in the corporate world today to entrust auditing to anyone who is not fully qualified. You need the best that you can hire. Auditing should *not* be a job for those without actual business experience, desiring to learn about the corporation. It should not be a classroom to educate new auditors. There is no substitute for experience and knowledge and we owe it to our stockholders to provide the best protection with the most competent audit staff possible. There is just too much at stake.

The selection of the audit teams should be the responsibility of the CGO or his or her staff. However, as you can see from above, there are certain requirements that must be met by individuals applying for internal audit positions. The prerequisites for effective internal auditors are:

> **At least five years experience within the corporation.** Having at least five years experience will be advantageous in two respects. First it will help auditors understand what the significant issues are in an audit relative to business consequences and secondly, it will be of value in gaining confidence from the auditee. The auditee, in many situations, will be an experienced manager, with audit reports being presented to them and sometimes being presented to their senior executives as well. There should be credibility in audit findings and recommendations. Many executives will have more faith in the validity of audit reports if they know that audit findings result from a foundation of extensive business experience. By analogy, there is a greater degree of credibility in a situation where an experienced teacher informs his or her principal of a student's behavioral problems and makes recommendations, than where recommendations come from a first year teacher who was experiencing difficulties with the student. This may not be fair, but it is in likelihood a reality.

> **Top performers.** You want the most qualified individuals to be internal auditors. You want the best of breed. The hours will be long, travel extensive, and you will want people who follow through on commitments and whose performance is above the mean.

> **Familiar with or having worked in numerous organizations within the company.** It is preferably, although not essential, for prospective auditors to have worked in numerous organizations within the corporation. This will give them a broader perspective of the integration and dependency of functions and processes that they are

auditing. As an example, if an auditor is familiar with both billing and accounts receivable and he or she is a member of an audit team engaged in a billing audit, then they should know the ramifications of erroneous billing to the receivables system.

➢ **Writing skills**. All prospective auditors must know how to write well. This is a prerequisite since top executives in most corporations review audit reports. Frequently, there are many levels of management reading and rereading the audit reports to understand them and the issues, and validating findings. The reports must be crisp, lucid and succinct. Badly written reports that are open to misinterpretation can result in a loss of valuable hours and resources.

➢ **Extensive backgrounds in controls**. It is helpful, though not essential, that audit prospects have knowledge of what adequate controls are and where they should be located. This knowledge can be acquired through audit education and training, either in school or on the job. Although I had spent more than ten years in my company before I joined audit, I was familiar only with basic IT controls. I attended auditing classes both inside and outside the company and acquired a fundamental knowledge of controls including, but not limited to, process documentation, preventive controls, detective controls and control points. My education was further enhanced by on the job training and spending my first audit year with experienced audit team leaders who educated me on the audit process.

➢ **Previous management experience**. Previous management experience is preferred but not essential. Having previous management experience can help you manage other auditors as you are given the responsibility of lead auditor. However, you could have acquired the leadership skills as a team or project leader in previous jobs. You can also develop managerial skills when given further responsibilities as you are assigned to numerous audits and work your way into auditor leadership roles.

➢ **Good team player.** This quality is essential, not just preferred. Although some audits are conducted by just one auditor, most are conducted by a team. Auditors work very closely with their fellow auditors, closer with their colleagues than they would with most any other assignment. Auditors travel with their fellow auditors and work closely with them for many weeks. In many instances they become like family; it is possible for them to spend more hours with their fellow auditors than with their actual families. They need to trust each other. Auditors rely on each other for support, coverage, knowledge and experience. Each auditor is part of a team and they must never forget that. The data that your fellow auditors obtain will most likely be closely woven with your own, with the end objective being a strong durable finished product. Auditors will depend on each other to share thoughts, information and ideas and being a good team player is a major asset. I have worked with auditors whose opinion and information I felt I could always trust. I have also worked with auditors who appeared to be loners, were not interested in being on a team and whose work was at times counterproductive, needing to be rewoven and retrofitted into the team's effort.

> **Expertise in at least one area of the company**. As I mentioned above, it is valuable for an auditor to have business experience and to be strong in at least one area of the business. When that area of the business is audited, the new auditor can be of significant value in understanding the processes and procedures involved in the audit. There is also a dependency on the understanding of interrelated processes, and as a member of an audit team, the individual who understands the process flows and interfaces can be a valuable source for their expertise and knowledge.

> **Knowledge of information technology**. There is a strong dependency on Information Technology within a company. There are few generated reports that are reviewed during an audit that are not IT generated. An understanding of the gathering of data, the flow of data, and the input and output controls as well as the processing controls and logic to generate reports and financial statements is a significant asset. Knowledge of information technology tools and techniques can be a great asset in today's audit world. Auditors should have a basic understanding of the IT world, as the integration and synergy of the IT and business world is more pronounced than ever before.

The size of the internal audit infrastructure that will be needed for effectiveness depends on the size of the corporation. Very small companies can probably fare well with a very small audit infrastructure, perhaps even one person, while large corporations can require a large internal audit department with scores of auditors. We do not want to overkill. However, we want a large enough infrastructure to be able to conduct frequent and thorough internal audits so that the board of directors feels comfortable that they have enough data to draw appropriate conclusions.

Now that I have discussed what I believe are auditor qualifications, what must the CGO and audit management do to maintain an effective audit infrastructure, once the audit teams are selected? It is my opinion that these are the areas that need attention:

➢ **Adequate Compensation.** Internal auditors need to be compensated well. The importance of their role is often understated, and young inexperienced auditors are hired who are paid minimal salaries. We should realize that the role the internal auditor performs is becoming more important than ever, and we need to adequately compensate to attract qualified, experienced candidates.

➢ **Rotate lead audit members**. Audit management needs to ensure that lead auditors are rotated. I have seen lead auditors get complacent and the quality of their work tapers off with each succeeding audit that they lead. A fresh pair of eyes and new leadership is sometimes needed to get a new approach. Rotating new lead auditors is also a way of trying to get the strongest possible auditor leading his or her field of strength. For example, if the CGO and audit management are planning the scope for an IT security audit, they might want to have the auditor who is most familiar and knowledgeable with IT security practices as their lead auditor.

➢ **Educate internal auditors on latest audit techniques**. Auditors should be schooled and kept up to date with the latest auditing techniques. There are constant changes in auditing techniques, especially in automated approaches that can be helpful. Automated approaches might help in obtaining better statistical samples and in even reducing audit time. Auditors should be encouraged to gain professional audit certification and should continue professional education.

➢ **Cross train.** Audit management should rotate their auditors for enhanced training. The more areas that an auditor learns and is educated in, the more valuable and productive he or she can become. I have been involved in audits where an auditor, relied upon for their expertise in a particular area, is suddenly removed from the audit and put on a special assignment, and the void has to be picked up by another auditor. Hopefully, there is a backup who has been trained in an area outside of their own.

➢ **Establish ceiling on length of service**. Audit assignments should be limited in duration. There are no steadfast rules here and there should be flexibility in determining each auditor's length of service. Many companies have a minimum length of service, but no maximum. The objective here is to avoid an auditor becoming burnt out and ineffective in their job.

Responsibilities of the internal auditor are to:

➢ Review, evaluate and report on the adequacy and application of controls. The reporting is formally documented in an audit report and distributed to executive management.

➢ Recommend control improvements and stress importance to improve overall control posture. These recommendations can be made at any time, but most frequently they are cited in formal audit reports. The recommendations should be reviewed with auditee management to alleviate future disagreements as to their value and merit.

➢ Advise management when an issue is closed and if recommendations made as a result of an audit are complied with. Many internal audit groups do not follow through on recommendations and leave it entirely up to the auditee to close the issue. Unfortunately, what I have seen occur, on too many occasions, is an assumption of closure by the auditee. As far as they were concerned, the issue had been closed with the implementation of corrective action. However, when external auditors returned to re-audit, they reexamined the issue to see if it was in fact closed. They concluded that implementation was not effective and in their consideration the issue was still open. Internal auditors have a responsibility to follow up on the corrective actions to their recommendations and certify, in writing, that they are satisfied and that there is closure.

➢ Determine the extent of compliance with internal business processes, ethical standards, and federal laws and regulations. Auditors have a responsibility to be familiar with standards, processes, policies, guidelines, and corporate instructions as well as with legal laws and regulations so that they are in a position to judge compliance.

➢ Assess the reliability and accuracy of data developed and reported with the company. Auditors should select sample sizes that are valid statistical samples, representative of the population. As a result of the sampling and testing done, the auditors should be in a position to extrapolate their results on the entire population, generating a comfort level with accuracy and reliability of data processed.

➢ Determine the protection of assets from possible loss. Auditors have a responsibility to review security as well as the controls surrounding company assets. Audits range from conducting inventory audits to reviewing the protection of classified and proprietary information that is important to the successful operation of the company.

➢ Internal auditors have another responsibility. They need to be involved in an advisory and educational role. They need to be there to assist in the design of controls, processing and procedures. They need to provide education if called upon by executive management. They have knowledge and expertise and as a result have a responsibility to be more than just examiners identifying control problems; they need to help prevent company wide control issues.

Organization Chart

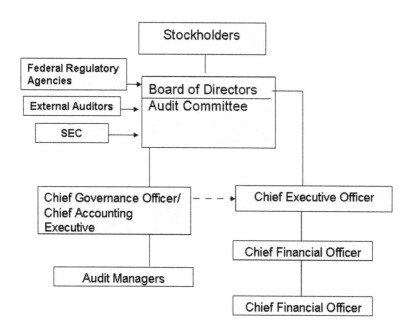

Summary

The intent of this chapter is to justify the necessity for a change in corporate audit infrastructures, abandoning old paradigms and focusing on a new reporting structure and qualifications of audit infrastructure members.

The audit infrastructure, the basis for the new audit readiness approach, must be fully supported and directed by an audit committee, selected from the board of directors. The audit committee must be totally independent to be effective. They must not own stock or stock options, or have other conflicts of interest. There must be rotation of the audit committee members, external-auditing organizations, and external auditing partners, and a close evaluation of the effectiveness of these groups. The audit committee must set policy and be responsible for establishing, distributing and monitoring compliance to a company's business code of conduct to ensure ethical behavior on the part of all employees. The committee is also responsible for selecting a chief governance officer who is totally independent and accountable directly to the audit committee. This executive will be responsible for establishing the audit readiness program and scope of internal audits, which need to be fully supported and endorsed by the audit committee. In addition, the CGO has the responsibility for the creation and continued effectiveness of an internal audit staff. Furthermore, there must be full cooperation among the CEO, CIO, CFO, other executives and the CGO for any audit program to be truly beneficial. In addition to an internal audit organization, there must be governance by external accountants and corporate counsel to ensure legal compliance to sundry government regulatory agencies and federal requirements rules and legislature.

The CGO and his or her staff must be loyal, trustworthy, and honest as well as experienced and educated in audit techniques and business processes. This is especially true with regard to knowledge of Information Technology as IT plays a very significant role in the generation of business and financial reports used to drive the direction and formulate strategies of our corporations in this highly technological world that we live in today. They must have the respect and admiration of corporate executives. Additionally, it should be recognized that internal auditors play a vital role and that they should be carefully chosen based on their qualifications and experience. They are the eyes and ears of the corporation and they should be compensated with attractive salaries, on an equal level with the top salaries in the company. This is essential and justified since it is through their efforts, that controls and sound business practices will frequently be recommended and the integrity and accuracy of financial and operational reporting will be evaluated and reported to the public, stockholders and outside regulatory agencies.

It is only through the establishment of a totally independent audit committee and board of directors; the full cooperation and harmonious partnerships of all internal and external organizations; and the existence of an experienced and dedicated internal audit infrastructure, that you can hope to achieve financial reporting accuracy, integrity and sound IT business controls.

Chapter Six

Proactive IT Control Activities

"Trust, but verify."

—Ronald Reagan

Introduction

The results of the audit in Chapter 4 were a total surprise to the CEO. The CEO was blindsided when Sally and John had 'an illusion of control' and gave the impression of being audit ready, but were totally unprepared. How many times have auditees been caught totally unprepared? Imagine yourself as a member of the audit committee having called the CEO in to explain what happened. He explains about being unprepared and you decide that you and the other audit committee members need to take action. But what do you do to avoid this problem in the future? Chapter Five mentioned that it is the CGO's responsibility to establish a program to achieve audit readiness. You sit with the CGO and agree that the company can not get caught in this situation again. You can not afford to have the CEO wearing the emperor's clothes: parading around naked thinking that he or she is appareled in the most magnificent attire. You need to have a pro-active program in place to help your CEO recognize when he or she does not have adequate controls. You need to have well controlled environments and you need to take pro-active measures to achieve this objective. People can no longer be trusted if they tell you that everything is all right. You can no longer trust what people tell you—you need to verify.

You ask the CGO to establish a pro-active audit readiness program that will verify and provide early warnings resulting in the implementation of corrective actions. The CGO and his internal audit department must help identify control problems and ensure that corrective actions are taken to correct identified control problems *before* an external audit takes place.

There are many activities that the CGO can initiate before official external audits are conducted to determine if there are, in fact, adequate controls established. These actions will include documenting processes, preparing flow diagrams with control points, writing procedures, conducting reviews, preparing self-assessments, and scheduling internal audits by your internal audit organization or by an independent external public accounting firm. These activities are pro-active in nature and play an important role in identifying where controls are inadequate, weak or missing. External SOX audits will identify where control exposures exist, either in design or execution, and recommend corrective actions to executive management.

Corporations however, can not wait for external audit reports to be written and distributed before action is taken. Self-assessments, internal audits, peer reviews, process documentation and procedures are an integral part of an audit readiness program. Management should be involved in audit readiness programs and attempt to identify as many issues and needed controls as they can *before* the CEO is told, as a result of an audit, that he or she has serious control issues.

The CGO should be held accountable to ensure that an audit readiness program is established to help identify areas where better controls are needed. While responsibility lies with the CGO, accountability lies with the CEO. The CEO is held accountable by Sarbanes Oxley legislature to ensure that adequate controls are installed and are effectively executed.

It is important to identify areas where controls are lacking or where controls are weak in order to understand where and what controls need to be designed into company processes. The pro-active approaches that I discuss can help achieve this. This chapter will be the initial step in helping you to understand what, where and when controls are needed.

The first step is to document your processes and procedures. You will need to determine if you have controls within your processes, and if not, to decide where they are needed. This is to be followed by an examination to determine if they are being executed effectively. But how do you know where you need controls or enhanced controls? There are various techniques that can be used to identify control exposures; it can start with a self-assessment.

Self-Assessments

No one is better able to assess his or her control posture than first line mangers and their key personnel. These are the individuals who day in and day out execute required process activities and are in the best position to identify potential issues, shortcomings or control concerns. Early warnings can be identified in self assessment questionnaires and can play a major role in establishing corrective actions, if done honestly and thoroughly. Unfortunately, I have seen three major problems with self assessments over the years that have negated their potential benefits.

- ➤ Self assessments are thought to function as a report card and *no one* wants to report failing grades.
- ➤ Self assessments are thought to be a nuisance and are not taken seriously.
- ➤ Self assessment questions are too general/vague and leave open many different interpretations of the questions.

If managers are asked to assess their control posture, they will most likely believe that if they bring forward issues, they are informing executive management of their own failures. Why should they admit that they are not prepared and that they have weaknesses? It makes little sense. The only exception that I have seen to this is in the situation of a new manager. Someone who has recently taken over a new department will want to know where his or her control weaknesses are so that they can be fixed. After all, they are the new player and have been hired to make improvements. In order to be successful when they take over the reigns, they need to know where any holes exist in their processes. I have seen new managers ask for their organizations to be independently audited so that they would know how much work and what work they will need to do. This is a strategic move that pays off for new managers.

But why rely solely on independent reviews by people outside your organization? As a new manager, you can ask your own organization to make—suggestions—as to where controls can be improved. One of the best tools to use can be the self assessment. The operative word here is *suggestion*. New managers need to encourage their employees to make suggestions and assure them that no-one will be held responsible. They have a new task, a new team and they can all win.

Now let's get back to the incumbent manager and fear of reprisal. It is a challenge, a difficult undertaking, to get an honest appraisal. Managers need to be told—and need to believe—that there will be no repercussions and that they are starting with a clean slate. They need to be apprised that it will be to their advantage if they find their own problems and clean their own dirty laundry as opposed to having an illusion of control and for someone else to cite their control exposures. This is a tough sell, but every effort needs to be taken to get the right message communicated to management for self assessments to be effective. Regrettably, I have seen the same scene played out numerous times: self assessments indicate that all is rosy or identify only minor concerns. Then an audit takes place and the auditors arrive at a different conclusion and identify major control issues. The executives scratch their heads, call everyone into their offices, read them the riot act and want to know how this happened. It's too late for everyone.

The second problem with self assessments is that not everyone takes them seriously enough. They are thought to be a nuisance and are really just a formality that needs to be done as quickly as possible so managers can concentrate on their real jobs. This is a fallacy that must be addressed. Having better controls in place will allow managers to do their job better. Managers need to be aware of this and the best way to stress this is with education and a demonstration that more efficient processes with tighter controls will eventually reduce costs and increase integrity. This is a daunting task but one that needs to be undertaken by the CGO and his or her staff.

I have seen too many instances where managers and their staffs answer 'not applicable' to self assessment questions when they thought the question did not apply to their organization or just did not understand the question. And I have seen situations where questions have been answered 'yes' when they should have been answered 'no' or vice versa, primarily because they were misunderstood. The CGO organization has the responsibility for addressing this problem. They are the ones who should design the self assessments for distribution and it is entirely up to them to deliver quality 'assessments' that are clear and understandable. I believed this was true for a long time but then realized that, as with any product, it is best to get the customer involved before you design a product.

The intention here is to design a general self assessment that will satisfy questions for all organizations and then to modify the basic self assessment with unique control questions that might apply to a specific organization. In my opinion, the most advantageous approach would be for the CGO to head a committee and solicit key managers to help design the self assessment. The committee of managers could propose their ideas for discussion and determine what questions would make the best sense. They should strive towards wording the questions simply and concisely, hopefully reducing misinterpretation. Once there is agreement on the general questionnaire, each manager would then have the option of adding their own questions that would help them address their own unique environment.

So let's take a situation where you are a manager of an IT department. The light has shone and you realize that you need to conduct a thorough self assessment of the controls surrounding your processes. You have a self assessment questionnaire that has been designed by a committee and distributed for completion. The self assessment is to be completed annually, except if you are a new manger. If you were a new manager, you would be asked to complete a self assessment within the first six months of your new position. Where do you start?

Let's take a look at the mechanics of completing a self assessment. Managers will be asked questions that can be answered either by "Yes" the control is in place, "No" the control is not in place or "N/A" if the control is not applicable. If N/A is used, the manager needs to explain why it is N/A. A valid reason for an N/A response might be if you are a DBA manger and you are asked if you add comments to source code documentation when application code changes are made. Since your department does not code application changes, the answer is N/A.

In addition, it is essential that managers indicate how they can verify that controls are in place. For instance, if they are answer "yes" to the question, "Is there adequate separation of duties?", they need to explain *how* separation of duties is accomplished within their department. If managers are not completing self-assessments themselves, but their staffs complete the assessments, management will still be held accountable for the answers. All self-assessments should be signed and dated by the manager of the department when completed.

An example of a very simple self-assessment questionnaire or checklist follows:

Control Question	YES/NO/NA No or NA—please explain	Yes—How was it tested? How can control be demonstrated?
Are processes adequately documented and key activities and controls identified?		
Can you demonstrate an up-to-date overall process flow for your process identifying the areas of risk and key controls?		
Are control measurements established to ascertain whether key control points are functioning properly and if the processes are effectively being executed?		
Are measurements reviewed with management, on a timely basis, and are appropriate actions taken to correct process weaknesses?		
Is there a plan to review processes to see where they can be improved?		

It would be in the best interest of your company to have individuals who have participated in numerous audits before, who can anticipate some of the questions, to be members of the design committee developing the self assessment questionnaire. It would be beneficial for the management committee, with the help of the CGO staff, to know what questions an auditor will ask, ask themselves these same questions and answer them before the auditor asks. Questions will be asked throughout this guide that could be candidates for inclusion in self assessments. Do not hesitate to include them. Other questions can be derived from the material that you will find spread out among the various chapters and they too should be considered for self assessment questionnaires. It is important to realize that the completion of the self assessment, if done well, will not only help you prepare for audits, but identify potential control problems with your processes. This is an opportunity to do more than just to prepare for an audit, why not take it?

Now as a manager how do you know how to respond to the questions? One way, if you are uncomfortable with just asking your staff for answers, is to conduct reviews before answering the questions, especially in answering those questions that focus on execution. These reviews can be conducted by peers.

Peer Reviews

There are many managers in your company who, when asked, will tell you that they have documented procedures and controls. And if they were asked if they were executing the procedures, they could easily say "yes". However, one of the best ways to know if procedures and controls are actually being executed is by conducting reviews. As Ronald Reagan said, trust, but verify. Managers should initiate peer reviews within their own departments to verify that a controlled environment exists. These reviews should uncover control deficiencies prior to internal audits and certainly before external audits are conducted. The reviews should help in validating that all self assessment questions have been answered honestly.

The reviews should not be limited to just self assessment questions but can and should be extended by the reviewers to whatever control questions they deem appropriate. The focus of these reviews is not only to determine if controls are in place but if they are being effectively executed. Managers should ask every member of their department to participate in peer reviews so that everyone's process execution is independently evaluated and no-one feels they have been singled out for a peer review because their work is being questioned. Again, education is important and all employees need to know the benefits and rationale of peer reviews.

Self-assessments and peer reviews are examples of management taking pro-active measures to identify problems before formal audits are conducted. Self-assessments and peer reviews are excellent methods to identify control deficiencies but they certainly are not the only method and the CGO staff stills need to verify answers and peer review results. A successful approach is to follow up self assessments with internal audits. Self assessments are usually completed by one individual within your department, peer reviews conducted by different personnel within your department and the internal audits by an independent group of reviewers who belong to the internal audit organization.

Internal Audits

Now picture yourself as the CGO. You have distributed self assessments and now have the responses in front of you. What do you do next? How much faith can you put into the answers? You need to assess the questionnaire results to formulate an opinion and to validate corrective actions. This is a crucial step in most corporations and should not be regarded lightly.

All completed self-assessments need to be collected and reviewed by the CGO and or their staff of internal auditors. Where answers indicate that controls are not in place where they should be, then the internal audit staff should request the manager to indicate what corrective actions, if any, the manager plans to take to ensure that controls will be put in place. If the manager feels that controls are not justified, or warranted, then that rationale should be documented and discussed with the internal audit staff. All action plans established as a result of self assessment questionnaires that identify concerns, need to be recorded and tracked until closure. We will discus this later in more detail.

The internal audit staff plays a key role and is the driving force behind an audit readiness program. They should be the catalysts for pro-active actions that will result in audit readiness. They are not only the driving force behind self assessments but they need to conduct internal audits on any process that the CGO or audit committee deems appropriate. They need to audit as many significant business processes as they can before external auditors conduct their audits and identify exposures. If there are too many processes to audit then internal audit needs to prioritize and audit those processes where exposures will do the most damage and where the company is at greatest risk. Internal audits need to be proactively conducted to thoroughly review the most critical areas of the business as well as reviewing self assessment answers and identifying control deficiencies where they exist *before* an outside accounting firm identifies the same weakness.

Internal auditors should identify control weaknesses and exposures and recommend how controls can be approved and how risks can be mitigated. With any internal audit there is a need to track management's corrective actions until closure.

The internal audit process will be discussed separately in the following chapter. In this chapter I discuss other pro-active measures that can help improve control posture and audit readiness. These pro-active actions are process documentation, procedures and control points.

Process Documentation

Ed Worsey is being audited as part of an external Sarbanes Oxley audit and the auditor asks him to explain his process. Ed verbally takes her through the complicated process that involves running the accounts receivables application, a stream of fifteen programs, with numerous backups, interfaces, special overrides, unique job streams at the end of every month, etc. The auditor then asks Ed how long he has performed the work he does and Ed replies, "twenty-five years". As a matter of fact he is planning to retire within the next six months because of poor health. The next day the auditor comes back to continue his review of Ed's processes but Ed has been taken to the hospital. Meanwhile, the previous night there was a problem during the A/R processing run. The accounts receivables input could not be read and no-one knew what to do. There were no instructions on what to do in this situation and how to recover. They wanted to call the accounts receivables manager but he was out of town and Ed never wrote down whom to call in an emergency. There is a scramble now to continue the run.

Fortunately Ed recovered in the hospital but unfortunately, much of what Ed did was not documented. He never found enough time to sit down and document his process. The department is in chaos. Ed knows every step of what he did but now someone else needs to step in and take over his responsibilities. The auditor is asked if she could come back perhaps next week because the department needs to see if they can continue to run the business smoothly. The auditor says sure, she understands and agrees that business comes first, but the next day indicates some significant findings in her notes. *"No existing operational process documentation for the company's Accounts Receivables system. Lack of process documentation or a documented run book caused a 24 hour delay in processing and a delay of recording $5 million in receivables."*

A business process is a set of repetitive functions executed to result in a predefined output. Every process should have a business process owner who is responsible for documenting the process. Documenting each process, describing how the process works, is an excellent vehicle for identifying where potential exposures exist and if controls need to be developed. If controls are documented, they can be evaluated to determine their adequacy and if they need to be enhanced and or modified. I have reviewed numerous process documentation efforts over the years and unfortunately controls are frequently missing from process documentation. They have not been documented, usually because they are non existent. Controls are frequently an afterthought and are usually not paid nearly as enough attention to as they should, until it is discovered that they are missing. It is important to realize that it is much more costly to design and implement controls *after* processes have been designed and deployed, than early on in their development stage. The earlier process documentation is reviewed in its life cycle, and the more management is likely to review the processes for adequate controls, the more likely potential weaknesses can be identified. Early identification can result in corrective action being taken earlier and lessen the likelihood of erroneous processing or uncontrolled activity.

Process documentation is one of the first requests that an auditor will ask for when reviewing a business process. Keep in mind that there are rudimentary steps that should be adhered to. These are:

1. Define the process and its measurements
2. Deploy the process and take measurements
3. Bring the process under control by eliminating variability
4. Analyze the cause of unusual results
5. Define process improvements and return to step 2

Process documentation usually consists of process narratives and process flows.

Process Narratives

Process narratives that I have reviewed or developed myself that I feel are very effective have included the following elements:

1. Process name.
   This is simply the process name that is generally recognized and associated with the process throughout the company

2. Process owner.
   This is the individual who has been assigned business ownership and whose responsibility is not restricted to process documentation. The process owner is also responsible to ensure adequacy of operation, effectiveness of control, timeliness of processing, quality of output, and accuracy of results as well as application security for those applications supporting the business process. Without a business process owner assigned and the responsibility accepted, there is a strong potential for the above responsibilities to *fall through the cracks*. I will expand on the role of process owners when I discuss Change Management in a later chapter.

3. Process objective.
   The objective of the process—its purpose—should be described. It is important to identify the scope of the process so there is little or no confusion as to where it starts or ends. When a company's business process descriptions are reviewed in totality and connected together, there should be a comfort level that business entities and business

disciplines have been described and that none have been omitted. Processes should flow smoothly, one into the other and should be interwoven to cover the business.

4. Roles and Responsibilities.

This process element addresses the roles and responsibilities of different organizations involved in executing the process. This may include operational personnel, IT personnel, HR personnel, financial organizations, managerial roles, staff roles, executive responsibilities, user responsibilities, etc.

5. Process description.

This is a detailed description of the process that should be augmented by the process flow that will be discussed next. This description should address *who* is responsible for the process, *what* the process involves, *when* it is executed and *where* it takes place. Do not try to answer the question of *how* it is implemented. This will be discussed later under procedures.

6. Input.

There should be a separate section in the process narrative that identifies all inputs (data and/or files) and their sources. It would be helpful if there were some description as to what processing is to take place with all input and when it is to be received.

7. Output.

Process outputs also need to be described. You will need to identify each output (data and/or files), when it is generated, its purpose, its classification and its destination.

8. Key events.

Identify what are considered to be the key events associated with the process. What triggers the process? How do you know that the process was executed effectively?

9. Control points.

You will need to discuss the control points in the process. A more detailed discussion of control points will follow shortly.

10. Business rules.

Every process should comply with business rules. It is important to identify what these business rules are.

11. Dependencies/relationships.

What are the dependencies for this process to be effectively and efficiently executed? Each dependency should be listed. Dependencies can be communication equipment, personnel, hardware, software expertise, experience, or interfaces with other processes.

12. Process measurements.

You should describe measurements in place for management to assess the effectiveness, timeliness and quality of processing. Process owners and users usually define measurements. You should also state how often processes are to be evaluated and by whom.

13. Process improvement plans.

You should detail any immediate or long range plans to improve the process and describe them here.

This list is not all-inclusive but it should give you a foundation for the composition of a process narrative.

Flow Diagrams/Control Points

As part of any process documentation, one can find it advantageous to create a process flow. There are various techniques that can be used that will identify where controls exist. These controls, indicated on the flow chart, should map to the discussion of controls in the process documentation. A control point is a time within a process that checking can be and should be done to validate that the process is being effectively executed. If we take as an example an Accounts Payable Process, control points can simply be a manual authorization of payments or an automated balancing program. Control points are also called exposure points. Exposures exist whenever data is:

- ➢ Collected
- ➢ Transcribed
- ➢ Processed
- ➢ Transmitted
- ➢ Stored

Auditors will be focusing on control points in an attempt to give themselves a comfort level as to how well processes are monitored. Following is a simplified flow diagram with control points for an "Issues Management Process" that follows the discussion above. It is followed by a process narrative. The type of flow diagram used is an example of what is referred to as "a swim lane flow diagram".

Swim lanes indicate the organization responsible for the function performed, the chronological sequence of events and a dependency relationship. You are not restricted to using the "swim lanes" or the process narrative format. This is only one example of what can be used. Most processes within the company will no doubt be much more complex and elaborate.

Process: *Issues Management* Frequency: *Monthly*

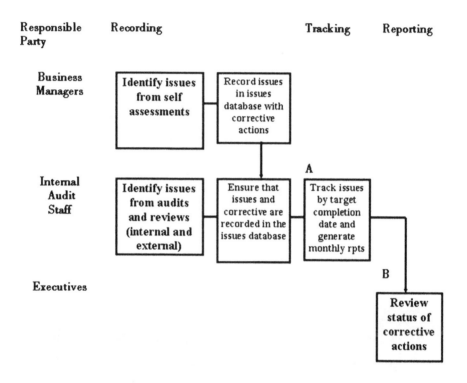

Responsible Party	Recording		Tracking	Reporting
Business Managers	Identify issues from self assessments	Record issues in issues database with corrective actions		
Internal Audit Staff	Identify issues from audits and reviews (internal and external)	Ensure that issues and corrective are recorded in the issues database	Track issues by target completion date and generate monthly rpts	
Executives				Review status of corrective actions

Process Name: Issues Management

Process Owner: Tim White

Process Objective: The objective of this process is to identify and effectively manage control issues emerging from reviews/audits, ensuring that they receive adequate focus, attention and resources necessary for timely resolution. The process addresses recording, tracking and reporting of issues.

Roles/Responsibilities: Management	1. Identify issues through management reviews and self-assessments.
	2. Record issues and corrective action plans with target implementation dates in an issues tracking database.
Internal Audit Staff	1. Identify issues as a result of any internal and external audits and reviews of self assessments.
	2. Have management record new issues in the Issues Tracking Database that were not previously recorded with corrective action plans.
	3. Track corrective actions target dates for completion and report status to the CGO monthly. The CEO and other executives should also be in the meetings.
Executives (CGO and Audit Committee)	1. Review corrective action plans to see if target dates have been met, and if not receive an explanation.
	2. Evaluate process to see if improvements can be made.
Process Description:	Issues that arise as a result of self-assessments, audits or reviews that can not be resolved within forty-eight hours should be recorded in an issues tracking database. They need to be tracked with corrective action plans and reported to the CGO and Audit committee until corrective action plans are implemented. Issues that can be resolved in less than forty-eight hours need not be formally tracked in an issues database.

Input:	1. Self-assessment issues 2. Audit report issues 3. Review issues 4. Issues raised by any manager
Output:	1. Issues recorded in the issues database. 2. Corrective actions recorded in Issues database
Key Events:	1. Identify issues 2. Record issues in issues tracking data base 3. Track issues and corrective action plans in issues tracking data base 4. Report issues to CGO and audit committee
Control Points:	A. Generation of status reports to track/record issues B. Review by CGO, audit committee and other executives
Business Rules:	Corporation instructions, standards, and guidelines
Dependencies	There is a dependency that all issues that are identified will be recorded promptly into the issues data base.
Measurements:	Objectives will be established for the percentage of corrective action plans to be resolved on target and measurements will be generated quarterly to track attainment of these objectives.
Improvement Plans	Process improvement plans are a possibility once the process is implemented and in place for six months. How can the process be improved with regard to timeliness, accuracy of processing and quality of output?

Procedures

Having process documentation without procedures is analogous to purchasing a new car without an owner's manual. You may know the process for changing a tire, but you may need a step by step procedure if you have never changed a tire before. Processes usually tell you *what, when,* and *where* but not *who* and *how.* Procedures describe 'how' to get from point 'A' to point 'B' and can usually be broken down into two levels. These are general procedures, sometimes referred to as 'high level' procedures and then 'detailed' procedures. High level procedures will inform the reader of the various tasks needed to execute a process while detailed procedures will describe 'how' each step is to be accomplished and by 'whom". Depending on the process that is documented, it may be sufficient to document high level procedures without requiring detailed procedures. The more elaborate the process, the greater the need for more detailed procedures. Auditors will ask for process flows, will most likely discuss process controls with you and will probably also ask for procedures. They may, or may not, 'peel the onion' down to detailed procedures but I have found that detailed procedures can be very helpful and beneficial in complex environments where there is frequent turnover of process personnel. Let's look at our rather simple process above and see what might be considered the supporting high level procedure and a more detailed procedure.

The process is 'Issues Management'. The high level procedure might be:

1) Conduct self assessments, audits and reviews.
2) Record issues and corrective action plans in an Issues Tracking Database.
3) Generate reports to see if issues have been closed.
4) Report corrective action status to executive management.
5) Executive management ensures issues are closed.
6) Implement process improvements if deemed necessary.

A more detailed procedure might be:

1) A management committee prepares self assessments with the CGO.
2) Internal audit and CGO distribute self assessments for management review twice a year.
3) Management asks staff to complete self assessments and has peer reviews conducted to validate responses.
4) Management reviews completion of self assessments, ensuring that all "YES" answers explain how testing was achieved and all 'N/A' answers indicate why they are designated as 'N/A'.
5) Management compiles all of their issues and has their staffs enter issues with corrective action plans into an "Issues Tracking Database".

6) Internal audit staff collects self assessments and ensures that they were all were received.
7) Monthly, the internal audit staff ensures that all issues that were identified have corrective action plans indicating who is to address the issue, and how it is to be addressed with a target date for completion.
8) Internal audit staff conducts internal audits, as requested, of business processes that are chosen to be audited by the CGO and executives.
9) Internal audit staff records issues in Issues Tracking Database.
10) Internal audit staff solicits corrective actions from management who were audited on their internal audit findings.
11) Management enters corrective action plans into the Issues Tracking Database for issues that Internal Audit has identified.
12) Internal Audit has quarterly reports generated from the Issues Tracking Data Base that indicates both closed and open corrective action plans with target dates.
13) Internal audit reports open corrective actions with target dates for resolution.
14) Internal Audit reports corrective action plans past due, aging them into 30, 60 and 90 days past due.
15) CGO, CEO and executives follow up with management to determine why corrective action plans are late.
16) On a semi-annual basis, the Audit Committee is made of aware of significant late issues that can lead to unsatisfactory audits or that have significant control consequences for the company.
17) Annually, the CGO and CEO evaluate the Issues Management Process to see how it can be improved.
18) Changes are made to the Issues Management Process (e.g., self-assessments) that are thought to improve the process.

As basic a procedure as this is, the purpose is to give you an idea of what a high   level procedure might be as opposed to a detailed procedure. There is another level below detailed procedures called 'desk procedures"

High level procedures are the link between the process that defines *what* and *why*, and a high level description that focuses on *how*. The more detailed procedure will focus on the *who* and *when*. Desk procedures are the procedures needed by each individual to complete their tasks. Desk procedures should be detailed enough so that if someone leaves their job, unexpectedly, someone else can step in the next day and follow the detailed procedure step by step until the job responsibilities are completed. It describes each and every step required to be fulfilled, peeling back the *who* from an organizational level to an individual level and the *how* from a general to a detailed step-by-step description of their actions. Depending on the process that is documented, it may be sufficient to document high level procedures rather than detailed procedures, or detailed procedures without desk procedures.

In the above process, an example of a desk procedure step for someone on the internal audit staff might be: "To support the Issues Management process please distribute the self assessments on April 1 and Oct 1 to the following mangers: Joe Black, Marsha Knight, Carol Seri, Bob Steel and Hanna Gnocchi and ask them to return completed self assessments within 14 days—file completed self assessments in your self assessment returned file."

Every process within a corporation should be documented with control points. Let us look at the classic Accounts Receivable flowchart that has been used for many years to give you more perspective. Although many of the steps reflect processes that are outdated, it is still effective as a teaching tool to illustrate the concept of flowcharts and control points.

Accounts Receivable Flowchart

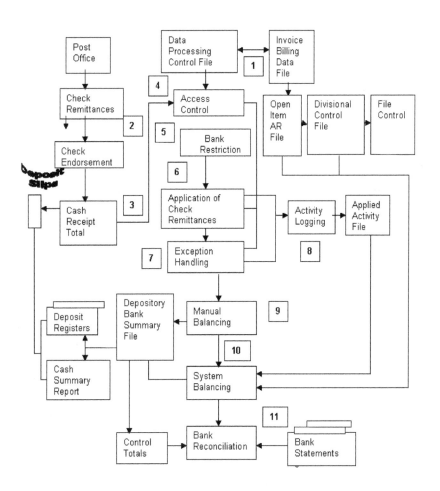

The numbers in the flowchart above refer to the following control points:

Control Point 1—Data Processing File Control

At control point 1, a divisional control file, which is a summary of the open-item accounts receivable file by type of accounts receivable (e.g. installment, net 30) is updated to reflect new billing data. A file control summary report is then generated to reflect the new updated file totals, prior to the processing of daily cash remittances. This control report is reviewed and approved by accounts receivable management at the headquarters location to ensure that the account receivable file and divisional control file are in balance.

Control Point 2—Check Endorsement

When the checks are received from the post office by the organization's branch office; they are given to a control desk, where a control clerk restrictively endorses them. This stamped endorsement "for deposit, company account, account number, date" prevents the deposit of the remittance to any unauthorized bank account.

Control Point 3—Cash Receipt Total

The control clerk then totals all checks and prepares deposit slips for each depository bank. This control is to ensure the accountability of checks received and their subsequent disposition. The receipted deposit slips and totals are filled in the branch office to be later reconciled to the daily cash (re: control point 9).

Control Point 4—Access Control

A security application, which controls access to all applications within the system, verifies that the operator is an authorized user of the system and that he or she is cleared for the requested transaction. Accounts receivable management may delegate or remove authority to process transactions but the security application limits management to the delegation of transactions within the scope of its authority and to transactions that will not compromise good separation of duties when processed in combination with existing transaction authorities.

Control Point 5—Bank Restriction

The choice of depository banks is limited to the specific banks identified in a branch office profile maintained within the accounts receivable system. This control ensures that the cash is being applied within the accounts receivable system to one of the depository accounts that may be used by the branch office.

Control Point 6—Application of Check Remittances

All check remittances within a batch must be applied to a customer's account unless the check remittance was erroneously sent to the company. If a check remittance for some reason is not entered into the system and is not subtracted from the batch totals the discrepancy will be highlighted in control point 9.

Control Point 7—Exception Handling

The Accounts Receivable system restricts the application of cash remittances to a single customer account. Only one customer account can be accessed for each check remittance. The entire check remittance amount must be applied to that customer account. The remaining check amount of one customer's payments can not be applied to another customer's account. A customer's remittance can only be applied if it is on the open item Accounts Receivable File. If it is not, then there is action taken to follow up with the customer. This could be a misrouted check by the customer. If misrouted, the check amount is then subtracted from totals and the check is routed back to the customer.

Control Point 8—Activity Logging

All cash remittance activity is logged on an applied activity file to provide an audit trail of transactions processed against the open Accounts Receivable File. The applied activity file is used in the daily balancing of the total accounts receivable system (re: control point 10) and for preparing listings that help in tracing lost activity that may have resulted from a system error.

Control Point 9—Manual Balancing

Manual balancing plays a significant role in our Accounts Receivable example. Daily, upon completion of application of cash remittances, the Accounts Receivable System prepares a cash summary report from the depository bank summary file. This report lists the total number of checks and total dollars applied to each depository bank for the day. The deposit registers are compared to the cash summary report to ensure that the cash applied to the system is in balance. In addition, the bank receipted deposit slips, referred to in control point 3, are reconciled to the cash summary report. This reconciliation ensures that the cash deposited in the specified banks was applied to the appropriate bank. After a control clerk balances the deposit registers and the summary report, management must review and sign. The deposit registers are filed with the day's customer remittances for future reference or reconciliation.

Control Point 10—System Balancing

In addition to manual balancing there is a dependency on system balancing. The two reinforce each other. The comparison of the applied activity file and the depository bank summary file ensures that all cash that has been deposited has been applied and recorded on the applied activity file. The computed total derived from subtracting the applied activity file from the divisional control file should equal the summary totals by type of Accounts Receivable of the current open item Accounts Receivable File. This system balancing imposes a three-way check to ensure that each file within the Accounts Receivable System is in balance. As a result, any out of balance condition is readily identified and appropriate corrective action initiated prior to proceeding with the next day's account receivable procedures.

Control Point 11—Bank Reconciliation

Monthly, corporate accounting management receives statements from the banks. These statements are compared to the totals that are transmitted daily to corporate accounting from the depository bank summary file to ensure that the depository bank summary file and the bank accounts are in balance. Any discrepancies in the totals are resolved.

I hope the Accounts Receivable flow above has given you a good idea of a flow diagram and its control points.

Independent External Assessments

Before a Sarbanes Oxley Audit commences, one of the most effective proactive measures and one of the last measures to take, is to have an independent assessment conducted by another public accounting firm. The additional external auditing staff would be engaged to review all of your documented IT processes and control design, and their execution. They would participate and collaborate with your internal audit organization to acquire knowledge of your business and ensure an understanding of, processes and controls. Once they have been educated, they would then conduct their reviews. Since they are familiar with SOX legislation and SOX requirements, and most likely have conducted SOX audits on their own, they can be an extremely valuable source. They would know what SOX auditors look for and could be a significant advantage as you prepare audit readiness. They would look at and suggest recommendations for improvement not only in the area of processes documentation and control effectiveness but also with regards to corporate governance. You will have the advantage of having expert feed back from a public accounting firm other than the one who will be conducting the SOX audit, while maintaining independence and separation of duties.

Once recommendations are made by the accounting firm that was hired to prepare you for a SOX audit, it is incumbent on you and your executive management team to ensure that all issues are recorded and evaluated to see if corrective actions need to be established. As with other pro-active measures, once it is decided that corrective actions need to be taken, they need to be recorded and tracked until closure. It can be expensive engaging the services of another public accounting's auditing staff to conduct audits prior to Sarbanes Oxley audits, but very beneficial. I have seen where this pro-active measure has uncovered additional exposures that were not recognized before. If an external review is being conducted by another accounting firm, a SOX audit should not take place until the accounting audit organization that you hired is satisfied that all of their recommendations have been remediated.

Summary

The internal audit department should assist management in conducting pro-active activities that will help identify control exposures. It is foolish to wait for internal auditors to conduct official audits to highlight problems, and certainly unwise to wait for external audits. Issues can be identified earlier as the result of pro-active measures taken by management. It is incumbent on management to know as soon as possible what exposures exist in their department and to correct the situation *as soon as possible*. To be able to succeed, it will be necessary for the internal audit organization to educate management on self-assessments, process documentation and flow charting techniques with control points. The effectiveness of self assessments as pro-active audit readiness tools is dependent on the quality of the questions and the 'honesty' of their completeness. It should be an objective of any corporation to produce the most comprehensive but simple self assessment questionnaires as possible using the expertise and experience from various management sources throughout the corporation. The questions must be understood and should cover as many potential audit questions as possible, and there must be no fear of reprisal if issues are identified. The more honestly the questions are answered, the less likelihood of illusion of control. We can not just trust, we need to verify. Therefore, it is incumbent on internal audit staffs to validate not only that the controls are in place but that they are being effectively executed. When you believe that all processes and controls are in place, a final pro-active measure could be to hire another public accounting firm other than your own, to review control effectiveness and identify any issues that exist. All identified issues still need to have corrective action plans recorded and tracked to ensure closure.

Another pro-active measure to be considered is to insure that every process is documented within the corporation with control points. The documentation should not stop here. Every process should have procedures (high level or detailed) and the procedures need to be executed.

The following information should be completed for each process and should help a company to be effectively pro-active.

1. What is the process name?
2. What is a description of the process?
3. Who is the process owner?
4. Does process documentation exist? What is the form (e.g., narrative, flow)?
5. Does the process have documented procedures?
6. Are there process control points? Are they on the flow or separately described?
7. When was the process last reviewed?
8. What type of review was it (e.g., peer review, internal audit)?
9. What controls were missing?
10. What controls were poorly designed?
11. Which controls had no evidence of being executed?
12. Were self-assessments conducted? When?
13. What were the results of the self-assessments?
14. Were plans put in place to address any issues?
15. What is the current status of these plans?

Chapter Seven

Assessment of IT Controls and Evaluation of Effectiveness

"Even if you are on the right track, you'll get run over if you just sit there."

—Will Rogers

Introduction

Let's assume that you have conducted self assessments, documented your processes, reviewed narratives and flow diagrams with control points, conducted self-assessments, evaluated peer review results, examined internal and external audit results, and reviewed independent external assessments by public accounting firms. You have in front of you pages and pages of issues and exposures that were identified. What do you do?

The words of Will Rogers must be heeded. You can't sit and do nothing when problems are found; they will not disappear. To do nothing is flagrant disregard of identified control issues and exposures and a neglect of blatant warning messages. A reluctance to take action will probably result in a reoccurrence of the problems and perhaps even greater exposure as time goes by.

The identification of control exposures resulting from audits, self-assessments and reviews has little or no value if not used as a foundation and basis for the establishment and implementation of corrective actions. To know where your problems exist and to realize what associated risks exist should you not take action, should instill urgency for the creation and implementation of plans that will minimize exposures. There are a number of steps that should be followed throughout this process.

When exposures are identified as a result of audits, reviews, or self-assessments, it is first necessary to validate that these exposures actually exist. Once validated, the issues that were identified need to be recorded. After they are recorded the risk to the business needs to be assessed and based on the seriousness of the impact to the business, corrective actions need to be developed, if necessary. The next step is to track progress on implementation of corrective action plans. Exposures and corresponding related corrective actions that are critical to the business need to be reviewed with the audit committee and corrective action status reported.

Validate and Record Issues

Each issue identified as a result of an audit, review, or self-assessment needs to be carefully scrutinized and validated. What is perceived and what was identified as an issue may not be an issue at all and there may not be an exposure. There may be other ancillary controls that were not revealed or uncovered but that may negate the exposure. There also may be mitigating controls that were not identified that could eliminate or reduce the likelihood of occurrence or business impact. It is important that line management validate each exposure.

Once issues are validated, they need to be documented and recorded. I suggest a centralized database to record and track all issues. All issues need to be recorded with indications as to when and where they were identified, brief descriptions, owner of issue, corrective action planned, target dates for resolution, and status. Access to the issues tracking database needs to be protected. Only authorized individuals should have access to the issues tracking database as it probably will contain proprietary information. Another item that needs to be considered is who should have read access and who should have update capability to the issues tracking database. Update capability should be very restrictive and you might want to grant update capability only to owners of the issues. Reports can be generated from this database for further review.

Risk Assessments

Once issues have been validated and recorded, the associated business risk needs to be assessed. The process of assessing risks requires insight and a business acumen that will result in good judgment.

There should be a formal business risk assessment process established in every company that is serious about their control posture and in preparing for successful audits. The risk assessment process should start with identifying the appropriate management who owns the risk. This is usually the owner of the process where the exposure was found. It is the risk owner who should prepare a risk assessment form. The risk assessment form should at least address the following elements:

> Definition of the problem
> Quantification of the exposure
> Development of alternatives
> Calculation of the financial impact for each alternative
> Selection of optimum solution
> Documentation of the decision
> Categorization of the risk
> Approval of the decision
> Revalidation of the risk assessment and decision

Definition of the problem. The first step in a risk assessment is to state the exposure or problem that was identified as the result of an audit, review or self-assessment that has been validated and recorded.

Quantification of the exposure. There are many factors that need to be addressed when quantifying an exposure. The owner should take into consideration:

➤ Impact in slowing the business down
➤ Potential or actual dollar loss
➤ Cost of recovery
➤ Time to recover
➤ Possibility of fraud or theft
➤ Probability of occurrence
➤ Probable duration of exposure
➤ Criticality to the business
➤ Cost of adding control
➤ Cost of alternatives

Develop alternative solutions. After quantifying the exposure, it will be necessary to decide on an alternative action. Options are:

➤ Continue with business as usual.
➤ Enhance controls that are already in place.
➤ Introduce new controls to the process.

Calculate financial impact for each alternative. The cost associated for each of the above alternatives needs to be calculated. This is a very important step and although not an exact science should involve as many individuals with the required expertise as possible. The cost of each enhancement or new control to be developed should be calculated.

Select optimum solution. The business decision as to which of the above alternatives one should select should be based on a financial impact. The cost of each alternative should be weighed against the financial impact of the business exposure. It is at this time that the risk is either accepted with the business to be continued as usual without a corrective action plan, or not accepted and controls enhanced or developed.

Document decision. The decision as to what action is to be taken should be documented within the formal risk assessment by the owner. The rationale for the decision should be explained.

Categorize the risk. The owner of the risk should categorize the risk as high, medium, or low based on an evaluation of what the exposure could cost the company in tangible and intangible losses. The category needs to be reviewed and agreed to by the owner's management and then by internal audit.

Approval of decision. Internal audit management should review and approve each risk assessment and decision made. The CGO should approve the actions taken on those risks that are considered high. High risks should be brought to the attention of the audit committee. Each risk assessment and approval needs to be documented and retained for audit purposes.

Revalidation of the risk assessment and solution. It is necessary to evaluate all risk assessments on at least an annual basis. The risk assessment process that is established for your company should indicate the time interval required for revalidation. Revalidation is necessary, as there might be changes in the environment, organization, company's position, economic situations, etc., during the interim. These factors might have an impact on the decision that was first made when evaluating the risks and actions; it may no longer be valid, hence the need for revalidation and reassessment.

The audit committee should review the company's risk assessment process and management's action plans to address significant identified issues.

Establish Corrective Action Plans

After risk assessments are completed, a decision is made as to the course of action: either to enhance existing controls or establish new ones. These two instances will require corrective action, as opposed to a third option: continuing business as usual without any action. The owner of the issue should develop the corrective action plan, if deemed necessary. A corrective action plan needs to detail the corrective action, state who is responsible for implementation, and set the target date for implementation. The person responsible for resolution of the issue is usually the owner of the risk. The owner of the risk may or may not be the same person who is responsible for implementation of the corrective action. The implementer might be an individual in the owner's department or another department who is delegated responsibility for resolution and closure. This information should be entered into the issues tracking data base.

Remediation Testing

Testing needs to be done after management has been told that action plans have been completed. This is necessary to validate that that the actions taken have in fact eliminated or mitigated the identified exposures. The results of validating corrective action resolution with closure dates should be recorded in the issues tracking data base.

Review with Audit Committee

Corrective action plans need to be reviewed by internal audit. Progress on the status of implementation plans needs to be tracked and reported to the

CGO, and corrective action reviewed with the audit committee if they are late or if they address high risk items. When these reviews are held with the audit committee, the presenter should be the line management in the organization that owns the issue and corrective action.

Assessment of Control Posture

At the end of the fiscal year, executive management, and the CGO need to assess their control posture and document their assessment in compliance to SOX legislative mandates. If there is agreement by the CFO and CEO that effective controls have been established and are being effectively executed, the next step is have the corporation's public accounting auditing firm *attest* to the adequacy of controls via an independent audit, as required by Sarbanes Oxley legislation. Whether or not a company is subjected to a SOX audit, every company should assess their control posture on at least an annual basis. This is good business judgment.

Risk Assessments on SOX Recommendations

If a SOX audit results in a "qualified report," the corporate executives need to examine the qualifications, determine the risk and decide if corrective actions are needed. The same procedure for recommendations made in a "qualified report" would be followed if recommendations resulted from an internal audit readiness review. This would entail issues being recorded, risk assessments performed, decisions documented, and corrective actions taken if necessary. The objective is to obtain an "unqualified SOX report." To achieve this objective, all actions and assessments need to be reviewed with corporate executives, and decisions and rationales documented and retained to discuss with the public accounting firm when they return, as they will, to determine if they can follow up with the issuance of an "unqualified report."

Executive Appraisals

It is important to integrate audit readiness and audit results into performance evaluations. Satisfactory control posture should be a component of corporations' executive staffs' compensation packages. The higher a percentage of their compensation is based on audit readiness, the greater an incentive it is for effective control design and execution. There is too much at risk not to incorporate audit results into executive appraisals. Corporations cannot afford to fall short, especially in SOX legislature compliance. CEOs and CFOs will be susceptible to punitive actions if they are not in compliance and corporations exposed to significant penalties. Therefore, audit committees should base their executives' salaries and bonuses on successful audits and corporate executives should hold their upper management responsible, tying all performance plans and compensation to satisfactory audit results.

Summary

There is little value in identifying problems without taking action to evaluate the risk, and making a decision to either accept that risk or to take corrective action. Before corrective action is decided upon, it is good practice to first agree that the problem exists. It is then necessary to perform a risk assessment to understand the extent of the exposure with regard to business impact, the likelihood of occurrence, the cost of fixing it, and what mitigating controls can be established, if any. If after a risk assessment it is decided to take corrective action, a formal action plan should be documented and logged. The corrective action plan needs to be logged and tracked until closure. The status of corrective action needs to be reviewed with the audit committee depending on its severity. It is important to review risk assessments and corrective action plans at least annually to determine if changes have taken place that mitigate the risk or make it more essential for corrective action to be taken.

It is necessary to ensure that executive performance reviews and compensation are directly tied to satisfactory audit results. This will put more weight onto correcting problems and in minimizing or reducing exposures

The questionnaire below should be helpful in assessing and evaluating issues and corrective actions that need to be established to address exposures.

1. Have all control issues been identified as a result of audits, reviews, and self-assessments?
2. Is there agreement by management that all issues are exposures?
3. Are all issues recorded in an issues database along with an indication of when and where the issue was raised?
4. Are risk assessments performed on all significant issues?
5. Have owners of all risks been identified?
6. Have corrective actions or risk acceptances been documented?
7. Has a determination been made whether corrective actions are needed to implement new controls?
8. Has a determination been made whether corrective actions are needed to enhance controls?

9. Which if any individuals are responsible for identified corrective actions?
10. Are the individuals reflected in the issues database?
11. Are target dates identified for corrective action completion?
12. Are corrective actions being tracked until closure?
13. Are tests conducted to ensure adequate closure of corrective actions?
14. Are risk assessments re-evaluated at least annually for continued business justification?
15. Are outstanding issues or significant exposures reported and reviewed with executive management?
16. Are corporate executives annually assessing their control posture as per SOX requirements based on what is reported to them?
17. Are executive performance plans and compensation based on successful audit results?

Chapter Eight

Internal Audit Process

"Facts are stubborn things; and whatever may be our wishes, our inclinations, or the dictates of our passion, they cannot alter the state of facts and evidence."

—John Adams

Introduction

Sarbanes Oxley Section 302 requires a company's management, with the participation of the principal executive and financial officers (the certifying officers), to make the following quarterly and annual certifications with respect to the company's internal control over financial reporting:

➢ A statement that the certifying officers are responsible for establishing and maintaining internal control over financial reporting.

➢ A statement that the certifying officers have designed such internal control over financial reporting, or caused such internal control over financial reporting to be designed under their supervision, to provide reasonable assurance regarding the reliability of financial reporting and the preparation of financial statements for external purposes in accordance with generally accepted accounting principles.

➢ A statement that the report discloses any changes in the company's internal control over financial reporting that occurred during the most recent fiscal quarter (the company's fourth fiscal quarter in the case of an annual report) that have materially affected, or are reasonably likely to materially affect, the company's internal control over financial reporting.

Under the new SOX rules, corporations cannot delegate responsibility to implement strong controls that ensure a reliable reporting system.

Company officers must create a system of control evaluation, and prepare an evidentiary report asserting the system's effectiveness. SOX states that merely instituting the control structure is not sufficient; company officers must also perform ongoing evaluation, identify any weaknesses in either the system or its operation, and be able to show the auditors that they have corrected any deficiencies. A qualified opinion from a public accounting firm conducting a SOX audit indicates that there are issues that need to be addressed. To avoid a qualified opinion, companies must complete testing and corrective measures well in advance of a SOX audit. Companies should establish a sound infrastructure spearheaded by an internal audit organization that will conduct ongoing evaluations and identify corrective measures. The process followed by internal auditors and management should be:

1. Internal auditors/management evaluate processes and control points.
2. Controls are enhanced where needed.
3. Internal auditors should conduct a review of processes.
4. Issues are documented.

5. Management establishes remediation plans.
6. Corrective actions are taken.
7. Step 3 is repeated until all issues are resolved.
8. External auditors are invited in.

Conducting effective internal audits is the most important role that the internal audit organization performs with regard to corporate governance of IT controls. It is generally accepted that the internal audit process should parallel the external audit process as closely as possible and be even more scrutinizing and demanding than an external review. Establishing an effective internal audit organization should help prepare you for any external audit. The value of an internal audit is to be as thorough as possible and try to identify any potential exposure. It is to your advantage that problems and issues are identified by the internal audit organization and corrected before external auditors arrive on the scene. As stated earlier, internal organizations are the eyes and ears of the board of directors and the stockholders. Among the most valuable products that an internal audit staff can be credited with is their assessment of the control and audit posture of the company and their help in preparation for any external audit. However, they should not be limited to conducting audits, which although is probably their most important role, should not be their only contribution to the company.

The internal audit staff also has another role, one of advisor and educator. They can and should 1) review all exposures (identified via self assessments, reviews or audits), 2) review corrective action plans and risks 3) provide advise as to what control points need to be inserted in various processes 4) help design control forms and 5) provide whatever control education is deemed to be beneficial to management. Their responsibility should not just be to identify and report issues, but to recommend corrective actions and do whatever they can to improve the overall control health in the company.

Internal auditors should not promote fear throughout the company. If auditors are to be effective in their jobs, they should be called upon by line management for advice and counsel and to help elevate managers' comfort level in the level of control within their organizations. They should be thought of as an essential organization by every employee of the company, as well as by the Board of Directors and company stockholders. I believe that the true value in being a member of an internal audit staff lies not just in participating in internal audits and deriving satisfaction from how many problems you find, but in moving outside the box, educating management to implement more effective controls and identify *significant* business and ethical issues. This includes understanding business risks and the ramifications that could result if issues are not corrected.

Many people are concerned with conflicts of interest if the auditor's role is expanded too far. How can the internal audit staff advise and assist in designing controls if they are also engaged in audits to evaluate their own recommendations and design? You need to ensure that different internal auditors are engaged in audits than those internal auditors who provide advice and counsel. This chapter will focus on the audit process that should be understood by all corporate executives.

The CGO should decide on the critical areas of the business that need to be audited. This should be reviewed and concurred with by the audit committee. Naturally, the audit committee can request that any area of the business undergo an audit, but for the most part, the audit scope should be decided by the CGO. Following is the process that the internal auditors should adhere to. *The process followed by the internal audit staff should as closely as possible resemble the process adhered to by external audit organizations.* You should be expecting a similar audit process to be followed when an external audit is conducted. Remember that the more closely the process exercised by your internal audit staff mirrors the audit process followed by the external auditors, the more prepared your company will be.

We should remember the words of John Adams: "Facts are stubborn things; and whatever may be our wishes, our inclinations, or the dictates of our passion, they cannot alter the state of facts and evidence." The auditor's role is to cite facts uncovered during the audit, identifying potential business exposures. There is no room in the audit process for guesswork and speculation. The following description of the audit process will hopefully extend the reader's knowledge of the process and minimize surprises encountered during the audit process. Whenever I use the term audit staff in this chapter, it can refer to any audit organization, internal or external, unless noted otherwise.

Kickoff meetings

Once the scope of an audit is agreed upon by the audit organization, an announcement letter should be sent to the auditee and executives within the organization being audited. A kickoff meeting should be scheduled by the audit organization and attendance should include audit management, the auditors conducting the audit, auditee management, and the auditee's key staff. The following items are examples of what should be presented by the audit staff:

➢ A brief overview of the audit organization
➢ The names of the auditors conducting the audit
➢ The name of the lead auditor
➢ The mission of the audit staff
➢ The audit reporting structure
➢ Protocols of the audit

> The audit process
> Status meeting schedule
> Expectations of turnaround on requests
> Audit reports

The following items should be included in an auditee overview:

> A high level view of the mission
> Key functions
> The auditee organization
> Audit contacts
> Name of Audit interface
> Any material or documentation previously requested that is available

---

Requests

Auditors usually say that that they will be as undisruptive as possible. In reality, there is little likelihood of finding an auditor who is not disruptive to your business. There is not much you can do to avoid this situation. Auditors, in order to do their job thoroughly, will need to be disruptive, to some extent. This will be true whether the auditors are internal or external. The more problems auditors find, the more requests they will make, the more questions they will ask, and the more disruptive they will become. Unfortunately, with regard to conducting day to day business, this is the auditor's MO and their disruption should be expected. The deeper they dig and the more they peel the layers of the onion, the more of a negative impact they will have on your being able to conduct business as usual. All requests should be responded to as quickly as possible. Expectations should be established during the audit kickoff meeting as to the expected turnaround time for supplying supporting information. Usually, requests are expected to be turned around within twenty-four to forty-eight hours. If there are reasons for delays in complying with the requests, the auditors need to be informed of those reasons as soon as possible. There may be extenuating circumstances that will need to be explained. Frequent reasons for delaying turnaround to audit requests are the absence of key personnel who are the subject matter experts in answering questions and in supplying requested information, or the urgency of addressing/resolving business issues that supersede audit requests. As an auditee, you will not want to appear to be non-cooperative with the auditor, and the auditor needs to understand the justification for the delay. The auditors will generally accept delay as long as there is reasonable explanation for it.

All audit requests should be made to and controlled by the individual designated by auditee management as the audit interface. All requests need to be logged and tracked. This includes indicating which auditor made the request, a description of the request, when it was made, when it was distributed within the auditee organization for resolution, who is handling it, and when it was responded to, and supplying a copy of the documentation. I have been involved in more than one audit where the auditor asked me again for information that I had already supplied, either because he or she had lost it, or because I had forgotten to respond to the original request and thought that I had. It is also not uncommon for multiple auditors to ask for the same documentation. There have also been situations where I have been accused of not supplying audit material as quickly as possible after explanations were sent to the auditor. Fortunately, I kept a log of correspondences. You need to keep control of the audit via logs for all communications. The audit can very quickly get out of control and the last thing you want is for communication difficulties to impair the audit process.

It is essential that there be a clear understanding on the part of both the auditor and auditee of what is requested. Failure of the auditor to clearly state what he or she wants and assumptions being made by the auditee on the requests can be counter-productive, with incorrect information being supplied. I can't recall how many times I had to go back and forth with the auditor when I was the auditee or with the auditee when I was the auditor, asking and answering the same questions and addressing misunderstandings. As I became more experienced as an auditor, my requests were made clearer and more concise. As an auditee, I made sure that I understood the auditor's request before numerous hours were expended by various personnel in responding to requests. This saved a lot of time and everyone benefited.

Auditors will probably request process documentation and procedures for those processes being audited. This documentation will probably be asked for prior to the kickoff meeting to allow the auditor time to read, digest and understand the processes that are to be followed by the auditee. If the auditee cannot supply this information prior to the kick-off meeting, they should bring it to the meeting.

Interviews

Auditors will most likely conduct numerous interviews, more than you would like. The interview process is critical to both parties' success. It is a kind of role-playing, and resembles a chess game, although there is a lot more at stake. The interview process can be a turning point in an audit, and it is important to know how the game is played and what is at stake.

The auditor asks key questions after he or she has had a chance to review the documentation supplied to them in answer to their request. He or she will probably concentrate on:

➢ Asking questions pertaining to the documented process to see if they understand it.

➢ Matching the documented process to the process stated in the interview, and probably looking for discrepancies.

➢ Focusing on control points during the interview, asking questions as to how the process is controlled.

➢ Asking questions pertaining to separation of duties.

➢ Asking the same questions during multiple interviews with different individuals to see if they get the same story.

➢ Stating during the interview if he or she has a concern with either a control being missing or a control that appears to be weak or not working.

From an auditee's perspective this is what auditee management should concentrate on:

➢ Do not leave inexperienced auditees alone with an auditee.
Have a manager or senior staff member present if possible at every interview.

➢ Ensure that notes are taken during every interview on what was said and what was asked.

➢ Advise all auditees, never to lie to an auditor.

➢ Advise the auditee that if they do not know the answer to an audit question, they should say that they don't know and suggest that they will get back to the auditor with more information after some research.

➢ The auditee should be told never to supply more than what is asked for and to only respond to questions asked. The auditee should not offer more information than is necessary to answer the question unless the information clarifies a point or could affect the conclusion reached (e.g., a mitigating control that was not obvious).

➢ Management or key personnel being audited should be advised to talk to the facts only. They should stay away from voicing opinions.

➢ Auditees should be instructed to ask the auditor at the end of every interview if the auditor has a concern at this point with any of the information that was supplied.

Interviews can be asked for at any time. Auditors will probably first ask for interviews after they have reviewed initial documentation. They may follow up with requests for further interviews to explain results of audit compliance tests validating the effective execution of designed controls. During the interviews, both parties should agree, if possible, on any potential exposures that might exist due to a lack of controls or non-compliance to a process. These concerns can also be addressed during status meetings, where findings are discussed.

It is interesting how many people fear auditors and hold back information. This is healthy up to a point. Auditors should only be given the information that they ask for. On the other hand, auxiliary controls that are used, even if not asked about, and rationales for actions taken or not taken based on prudent business decisions, should be discussed with the auditors. An audit is a two-way street. It is a give-and-take process for both auditee and auditor. It should be a beneficial exercise, advantageous to all parties and a "value add" for the company.

Findings

You are the CEO and your accounts receivables process has just been audited. Dave and Mary, your external auditors, as part of their IT Sarbanes Oxley audit have just finished their review of the accounts receivable application monitoring process and documented the following finding:

"213 million dollars of accounts receivable revenue was recorded during the 6 month audit time period from January through June. Message errors that were generated during this audit time period were not resolved in a timely fashion. This resulted in delays of recording revenue during this period."

This finding was sent to your auditee management for review. Was it accurate? Yes, it was. Was it misleading? Unfortunately, yes. The findings do not state how many error messages were generated during this period, what the error messages were, the percentage that were not corrected in a timely manner, nor the delay in correcting the errors. All of these additional facts were important and should have been included. It's true that there were error messages, but additional wording should have been added to make the reader understand the impact of the problem. There were nineteen error messages generated during this period. Eleven were warning messages that were not really application error messages and did not prevent records from being processed. They had to do with potential space problems as the number of records being processed increased. The messages read, "Disk space approaching capacity investigate future potential capacity concerns." Were these processing errors? No. Of the other eight that were valid processing errors, six were corrected within the service level agreement of twenty-four hours and two, for five thousand dollars, in combined revenue, were delayed for an additional twenty-four hours. They were tracked, recorded and resolved as soon as the subject matter experts, who were engaged in resolving system outages, were available to work on them. Should these facts been included in the finding as well? You bet they should have been, as this finding was used in the final report and presented the readers, including many executives with a wrong impression of the seriousness of the problem. The reading, reviewing, and concurrence with the wording in the audit findings by auditee management are crucial.

The above scenario could take place during an internal audit, if the internal audit is truly preparing the auditee for an external audit. Auditors should have questions as they review the process documentation, hold interviews, and review compliance tests, or when ensuring that the processes are being followed. Questions that are not answered to their satisfaction will result in audit findings. These findings need to be discussed with the auditee and auditee management. If agreement is reached that there is actually a finding, then the finding needs to be documented. Once documented, the finding again should be closely examined by the auditee. It is here that the finding needs to be read very carefully and agreed to by both parties before going forward. It is the documented finding that will find its way into the final audit report so there must be agreement. As an auditor, I tried to get sign-off and agreement from management on the finding that 1) they understood the issue and 2) that it was accurately stated. This saves a lot of time. I didn't want the auditee to tell me, after the final report was written, that they did not agree with the findings or ask me how I could possibly believe what I stated the issue to be. As an auditee, this was one of the most important responsibilities I had. It was imperative that I read the finding and made sure that I agreed with the facts. If it did not tell the whole story, I would ask the auditor to add more, especially if there were mitigating circumstances or auxiliary controls, not necessarily documented, but executed. I would also ask the auditor to state if the business impact of the control or process was weak or non-existent. I needed to understand the business risk of not having the control in place. I experienced many audits where the findings were thrown out or significantly reworded, clarified, or weakened, regarding the business impact *after* the final report was written. This resulted in a waste of time on both sides. These issues should have been addressed when the findings were documented. There was additional work required by the auditee and unnecessary executive involvement on the part of the auditee organization once these issues appeared in the final report. For all parties involved, this process in the audit needs to be as professional as possible. The documented findings will often go back and forth for some time, with revisions and explanations being added until agreement is reached.

Status Meetings

Findings should be reviewed and agreed to during status meetings, after all information is digested, and *before* the final report is written. Status meetings can be held daily, weekly, semi weekly, or biweekly. They can also be held whenever there is need to discuss potential findings or the audit status. This is especially true if there was evident fraud or significant material exposure. Both audit management and auditee management should attend status meetings, as well as the parties directly involved. The auditor should schedule the status meetings and invite the auditee and whomever else they feel should be in attendance. Minutes should be generated from the status meetings and distributed to ensure concurrence on what was discussed, and issues identified.

Recommendations

The auditors will make recommendations to the auditee based on their findings. These recommendations do not have to be agreed to by the auditee but many auditors will try to get the auditee's concurrence if possible. The auditee must respond to the recommendations and it makes the entire process smoother and less painful if there is agreement early on in the audit process and not susceptible for debate, after the audit report is written. Recommendations must make good business sense and I have witnessed the value of more experienced auditors as the business impact needs to be known before a valid recommendation can be written. An auditor with years of business experience and business acumen is in a better position to understand business impacts. Again, the objective here is to use good judgment and sensitivity, and be considerate about time. An auditor must never forget that the first priority should be to keep the business running and that time is valuable and should not be wasted. It is the auditor's responsible to make the most valuable recommendation that he or she can make. As an auditee, you have a responsibility to review the recommendation and to discuss it with the auditor especially if you feel that it does not make sense. Your management team will be responding to the recommendation with action plans and you do not want time to be wasted.

Final Report

The final report is the summation of the audit process. It is the culmination of days or weeks of investigations, reviews, and meetings. The final report should have an introduction that explains the process being audited and the individuals responsible. Each finding should be clearly stated. The wording in the final report should be the same as the wording in the findings previously written and reviewed. Each finding should have a recommendation that was also previously reviewed. The report is then distributed to the company executives including the CGO. The CGO need not get involved prior to this point unless:

> ➤ There are significant exposures or evidence of fraud or financial misrepresentations.
> ➤ There are disagreements by the auditee executive management on the final report and they refuse to sign off.

What needs to be reviewed with the audit committee is up to the discretion of the CGO, but only after he or she discusses the audit results with the CFO and CEO. If appropriate, the CIO and CSO might also be included in reviewing audit findings affecting security policies and or IT controls. It might also be advantageous to include general counsel in audit result discussions when there are any legal questions or concerns. The benefits in this approach will be that when the CGO presents audit findings that are felt to be significant to the audit committee, there will be no surprises among the executives.

I personally would recommend that every unsatisfactory financial audit and every audit that identifies significant control weaknesses, security exposures, ethical misbehavior, or non-compliance to federal laws be candidates for discussion with the audit committee to determine what action will be taken and by whom.

Final Audit Report Distribution

The final audit report is usually distributed according to a formal distribution process. The report is usually sent to the auditee management and their executive management as well as to the audit management team and their senior management. Other individuals are added to the distribution list as deemed appropriate. For example, if there is evidence of fraud or misappropriation of assets than the auditee's legal organization will probably be a recipient.

Final Audit Report Response

When the final audit report is distributed there is usually a request for the auditee to respond to the auditor within a specified time period. The response should state what corrective action will be planned, who is responsible for the corrective action, and a target date for completion.

It is important for the auditee to understand the risk of not complying with the recommendation made by the audit staff. Not every recommendation will have a corrective action that will be cost justified, nor does every recommendation need to be accepted. Some exposures identified in audit reports will not be worth-while for the company to correct. The risk may not warrant the cost of corrective action indicated. If this is true, an analysis should be performed and included in the response to the auditors.

The individuals on the distribution list should be copied on the responses. Auditors have the option of either accepting or rejecting the audit response and this decision should be documented. Auditors usually come back and revisit the issues and corrective action plans that were identified. They pay particular attention to previous audit issues to validate that they have been addressed, and if not, to understand why.

Summary

The internal audit organization should focus on weakness in controls and/or business processes. This is essential if you desire effective corporate Auditing Information Systems and Controls resulting in successful audits. The internal audit process should map closely with external audit processes and that should be an additional benefit. The internal audit should be performed by experienced auditors with years of business experience. As a result, the findings should be more extensive and comprehensive and the recommendations of greater value. For the internal audit process to be truly effective, it will require 100% cooperation on the part of the auditee. If the findings are valid and significant, the company will benefit by taking corrective actions in response to audit recommendations. Internal audits, if performed well, will be a plus for all concerned and will help everyone understand business impacts of exposures and the corrective actions that need to be implemented.

The internal audit process should map as closely to the external audit process as possible. The process begins with a kick-off meeting where the scope is discussed, followed by audit requests for information and data, audit field work where findings and recommendations are written, and the finalization of audit reports. It is the responsibility of the CGO to review significant audit findings with other executives before reviewing the issues with the audit committee. These reviews should be held with the CEO and the CFO, and potentially the general counsel, CIO, and CSO if appropriate.

The audit process will be the same for whatever process is being auditing, what will change are the checklists and questions being used. It is critical that management understand the audit process and pay particular attention to the findings that are documented and review them for accuracy. The findings will be the basis for the final audit report. Auditees should ask the auditors to include any additional or extenuating circumstances related to the findings that will help the reader and executives understand the magnitude of the problems and business impacts. The auditee will have an advantage during an audit if he or she understands the audit process.

To prepare auditees and internal auditors for audits, the CGO should ensure that:

➤ All potential and current auditees understand the audit process, supplying education if necessary.
➤ An announcement letter is received before all audits.
➤ Key personnel attend the audit kickoff meeting controlled by the auditors.
➤ Auditees establish audit interfaces.
➤ The internal auditor asks for documentation before the kick-off meeting.
➤ Audit roles/responsibilities are discussed at the kick off meeting.
➤ Auditee management is present during all audit interviews.
➤ Issues are identified during the interview process.
➤ All audit requests are turned around in the requested time, or the auditor notified if problems arise.
➤ The auditee logs all audits requests.
➤ The auditee reviews all findings for validity and misleading statements.
➤ The auditee understands the business impact or risk if the control identified by the auditor is weak or nonexistent.
➤ The auditee reviews all findings for clarity.
➤ The auditee suggests clarifications to the findings, if necessary.
➤ The auditee works with the auditor to review acceptance of suggested word changes.
➤ The auditee reviews recommendations.
➤ The auditee ensures that the recommendations make sense.
➤ The auditee makes the auditors aware of any concerns with the recommendations.
➤ The auditee reviews and understands the final report, although he or she does not have to agree with the recommendations.
➤ The auditee responds to the audit recommendations in a timely fashion.
➤ The auditee documents corrective action plans and keeps track of progress until closure.

Chapter Nine

Sarbanes Oxley Audit Process

"The things that hurt, instruct."

Benjamin Franklin

Introduction

The requirements imposed on corporations by Sarbanes Oxley legislature have necessitated the establishment of strong internal audit infrastructures to position executives to comply with the new regulations. Sarbanes Oxley requires corporate management to identify, document, and evaluate significant internal controls and to evaluate the operating effectiveness of controls within their organizations. They cannot use inquiry alone to assess their control postures nor can they delegate these responsibilities to outside auditors. There can be considerable cost involved in compliance, but this cannot be avoided. The rules have changed under SOX, not only for corporate governance by an entity's internal organization, but for public accounting firms conducting external audits as well.

Separation of Duties

In the previous chapter I stated that internal audit organizations can fulfill a role of providing advice and counsel to their executive officers, as well as conducting IT audits, but that they need to preserve their independence; it is a thin line. If there are personnel within the internal audit organization who are providing an advisory role (e.g., reviewing design of controls and recommending changes, if needed), then they should not be the same personnel who engage in auditing the same controls. You must maintain separation of duties. This is true even to a greater extent when we refer to public accounting firms who are your external auditors. Your external auditing firms should not provide assistance in designing controls. Executives should not look to them for guidance in implementing, evaluating, or strengthening controls. Under the Sarbanes-Oxley Act, auditors are severely limited in how much help they can provide. The assistance provided by public accounting firms must not interfere with their independence. You must avoid conflict of interest. Many companies today hire a second public accounting firm, in addition to the firm conducting the Sarbanes Oxley Audit, to independently review and evaluate controls and to recommend control design improvements to prepare them for SOX audits. I have even seen instances where an outside audit firm was retained by a corporation to work with an internal audit organization and assist in conducting internal audits. This was discussed in the previous chapter. This is acceptable as long as they are not conducting Sarbanes Oxley Audits.

SOX 404 Requirements

Public accounting firms have more skin in the game than ever before and are exhibiting more caution, more prudence, and more deliberation before conclusions are reached. They are more reluctant to attest to adequacies of corporate control structures and their effective execution without a higher degree of comfort than they might have had in the past. They are more hesitant than ever before and are certainly more thorough in their audits. They want to assure themselves that they are covering all bases. Sarbanes Oxley has changed the game and the stakes are higher. No public accounting firm wants their image to be tarnished. They are concerned about their reputation, especially after Arthur Anderson's collapse, and do not want to follow suit. There are more eyes on audit activities and more expectations on the quality of audit reports than ever before, both by the public as well as by the SEC. Public accounting firms are more wary of their auditing practices, and who can blame them?

To repeat what I mentioned in an earlier chapter and set the stage for this discussion, section 404 of Sarbanes Oxley is the basis for discretion evidenced by public accounting firms during their audits. Section 404 of Sarbanes Oxley went into effect in the year-ends beginning on or after November 15, 2004. The directives of Sarbanes-Oxley section 404 require that management provide an annual report on its assessment of internal control over financial reporting in the annual filing. It states:

Management's report on internal control over financial reporting is required to include the following:

> A statement of management's responsibility for establishing and maintaining adequate internal control over financial reporting for the company.
> A statement identifying the framework used by management to conduct the required assessment of the effectiveness of the company's internal control over the financial reporting.
> An assessment of the effectiveness of the company's internal control over financial reporting as of the end of the company's most recent fiscal year, including an explicit statement as to whether that internal control over financial reporting is effective.
> A statement that the registered public accounting firm that audited the financial statements included in the annual report has issued an attestation report on management's assessment of the company's internal control over financial reporting.

As we can see, the bar has been raised for public accounting firms. PCAOB Auditing Standard No. 2 provides definitive guidance on how auditors should evaluate internal control deficiencies. Standard No. 2 strongly suggests that auditors use the COSO framework as guidance for control evaluation. The COSO framework requires that the following components be adequately addressed for an entity to achieve effective internal controls:

> ➢ The control environment
> ➢ Risk assessments
> ➢ Control activities
> ➢ Information and communications
> ➢ Monitoring

SOX auditors will probably first determine if corporations are satisfying the components that are stated above. SOX auditors must review management's assessment of their control posture and then, as a result of their own thorough testing, evaluate control design and effective execution. They will review the controls that management indicates have been established, review the framework in place, gain an understanding of how management assessed their control design and effectiveness, and then validate management's assessment via an attestation report.

Similarities to Traditional Audit Process

There are many similarities between SOX audits and traditional audits that are either conducted by internal audit organizations or external auditors. The following items that were discussed in the previous chapter as components of traditional audits will be integrated into SOX audits as well:

> ➢ Kick-off meetings
> ➢ Requests for process documentation and procedures
> ➢ Interviews
> ➢ Findings
> ➢ Status meetings
> ➢ Recommendations
> ➢ Final report

Differences with Traditional Audit Processes

However, even though basic audit process fundamentals are relatively unchanged, there are still differences between traditional audits and SOX audits. Some of the more noticeable variances occur in the following areas:

Audit Commencement

SOX audits are conducted *after* management has assessed their control design, tested control execution to their satisfaction, and concluded that they are ready for a SOX audit. Corporate executives must first assess the effectiveness of their internal controls for the fiscal year as a result of in-house testing; the executives must document a statement as to the effectiveness of controls, as per SOX requirements. Corporations will decide if and when they are ready for an external SOX audit that will attest their assessment that their controls are effective. Corporate executives' actions and audit readiness will be the trigger for SOX audits. A SOX audit *will not* take place until corporate management and internal audit control organizations assess their readiness. This is not necessarily true in the case of traditional or non-SOX audits where regularly scheduled audits are conducted and auditors assess the control design and effectiveness of execution, whether or not corporate management have first conducted their own preliminary reviews and assessed audit readiness. There is more dependency on management to identify, document, and evaluate significant control issues and to remediate any significant issues *before* a SOX audit commences.

COSO Framework

The SEC strongly recommends that SOX auditors use the COSO framework as a guide in evaluating control effectiveness and control adequacy. If COSO is not used, then a similar framework should be used in its place. The important point is that the processes and controls that are going to be tested by SOX auditors in their fieldwork are the very same processes and controls that corporate management has indicated that they use and have been assessed by their internal organizations. There should be no surprises during a SOX audit with regard to what the auditors will be reviewing. SOX auditors will work very closely with the internal audit organizations to understand and review the documentation of established processes and key controls and to review the results of in-house testing. The auditors will evaluate the identification and placement of key controls, and they will then conduct their own testing of these controls to attest to adequacy of execution. This was not always true during non-Sox external audits that I was involved with, where control questions were entirely up to the discretion of the external auditors and might even have been a surprise to auditee management during the audit. On numerous occasions, I have been witness to situations where auditors expanded the scope of the original areas they were reviewing because they found suspicious activities that led them to ask other questions and even to evaluate other processes that were originally out of scope. I evidenced this "scope creeping" at various times and I was guilty of scope creeping myself when I was an auditor. Scope creeping is much less likely during a SOX audit as the scope is predetermined by all parties.

Control Focus

SOX interviews will focus equally on preventive and detective controls that have been implemented. Traditional or non-SOX audits usually focus more on detective controls. If we go back to our definition of detective controls, we should remember that detective controls are controls that reveal or discover unwanted events after they occur, as opposed to preventive controls that prevent fraudulent or erroneous processing before they occur. During interview sessions, SOX auditors will ask questions in an attempt to match the preventive and detective controls to the process flows that they were presented with, to see where in the process flows these controls reside and to test their effectiveness. As I stated earlier, the focus will be on key controls, those controls that are most significant in preventing and detecting erroneous or fraudulent processing. Unfortunately there is usually not enough time during the audits to focus on all controls so the primary attention will be placed on those deemed to be key controls.

Financial Applications

SOX auditors will primarily focus on financial applications but they will not necessarily limit themselves to this application group. They may also review feeder applications that send data to financial applications, considering these to be 'critical' applications. The auditors will look to see what controls from a transaction viewpoint have a direct effect on financial statements, and will focus more on these transactions, wherever they reside, and not necessarily confine themselves to a list of financial applications. However, keep in mind that even if the scope has been narrowed and fewer applications are audited in a SOX audit than in a traditional audit, assuming that there were more non-financial applications that were audited before, the SOX auditors will be more intense and thorough during their audits. SOX audits are fundamentally finance oriented, as the impetus for SOX legislature were the financial scandals of the 1990s. The realization that IT plays a significant role in financial reporting and business processing has led to greater focus on IT based audits. SOX auditors will still audit the control environment during financial IT audits. For example, they will audit development methodology, risk management, and management's awareness and involvement, as well as management's assessment.

Reliability

Findings will result from field work using the COSO framework as a guideline. The field work will be more complete than traditional or non-SOX audits. SOX auditors will be looking for reliability. They will look for effective execution of controls throughout the audit period and not just at the time of the audit. You will need to demonstrate reliability and consistency of effective control execution throughout the entire audit cycle, which should cover the fiscal year. SOX auditors are attesting to the sustained effectiveness of control execution and not the control status at just a point in time. When the SOX report is issued, the readers will want to know if they can rely on controls that are well designed and are being effectively executed.

Findings

There are no grey areas during SOX audit field work. Either controls are effectively being worked, or they are not. If issues were identified during traditional audits and management was able to demonstrate that they had implemented corrective action plans a few weeks prior to the auditor's arrival, the auditors would probably not have written them up in their findings. Additionally, if management had corrective action plans documented but had not implemented them before the audit, the auditors might have credited management with having corrective action plans documented and recommended that they be implemented as soon as possible. Traditional or non-SOX auditors are more likely to give management credit for having established corrective action plans that are in the process of being executed, or to give them recognition if execution of corrective actions was recent. This will *not* be true with SOX audits. SOX auditors will need to validate the execution of controls for the *entire audit period*, not partial implementation or plans for implementation. They need to attest to the effectiveness of controls. It is either "yes" or "no": either they can attest to management's assessment that controls are effective and have been effective throughout the audit period—or they cannot.

Secondary Controls

During audit interviews SOX auditors might ask about secondary controls or manual controls that might be in place, and focus more on risk management and executive awareness of potential risks that might exist due to control deficiencies. SOX requires corporate management to be aware of their control posture, to have assessed their control posture, and to have put secondary or mitigating controls in place that will reduce risk where issues have been identified. These secondary controls should be accepted by SOX auditors if they can be shown to be reliable and effectively executed for the entire audit cycle.

Overall Opinion

I am constantly being asked by auditees after an audit, "What was the rating?" "Did I pass or fail?" Traditional or non-SOX audits are usually rated by the auditors as *"satisfactory"*, *"marginal"*, or *"unsatisfactory."* *Satisfactory* means that there are no significant errors, *marginal* means that there are issues that if not addressed could lead to unsatisfactory audits, and *unsatisfactory* means that there are significant exposures that have resulted in actual or potential material losses. SOX audits reports and overall opinions in the reports are different from traditional audit reports. The SOX final reports will not have satisfactory, marginal or unsatisfactory ratings. The reports will be an "attestation" of the effectiveness of the controls that are in place. The controls are either satisfactory or not. Auditors will have a "qualified" opinion if they find significant deficiencies or material weakness. If a significant deficiency or a material weakness is found, it will preclude an "unqualified" opinion: that controls are effective. Significant deficiencies are control exceptions such as weaknesses in general design or control operation. It is important to realize that numerous control deficiencies, which by themselves would be insignificant, when combined with other deficiencies could in totality have a common feature or attribute that will elevate them to another level of significant deficiency. You should realize that the SOX auditors' opinions of and willingness to attest to the effectiveness of the *overall* control posture and not just to *each* control component could result in a report with qualifications.

In a SOX audit you do not want qualifications. The auditors will be stating an opinion after they review the designs, executions, and management governance, and you will want a report without qualifications. If there are qualifications, there will be recommendations on corrective actions and the public accounting firm will have to return to conduct another audit after remediation and render another report attesting to the adequacy of controls, this time—it will be hoped—without qualifications.

Summary

When we look at the Sarbanes Oxley Audit and compare it to the traditional or non-SOX audit, we realize that there are both similarities and differences. There are higher standards that have to be attained than ever before and SOX auditors are being measured against these elevated expectations. SOX has raised the bar both for corporate executives, who are responsible for establishing and maintaining adequate internal controls and assessing their effectiveness, and for public accounting firms, who conduct external audits and who are responsible for an attestation report on management's assessment of their company's internal control.

Public accounting firms who are responsible for validating control assessment must ensure that they maintain independence and do not find themselves engaged in activities that will place them in a separation of duties quagmire.

SOX auditors are reluctant to attest to the effectiveness of controls without conducting more thorough audits than they had in the past. They are working closely with internal audit staffs and management teams to review corporations' established processes, controls, and frameworks, using the COSO framework as a guide to validate and attest to management's self-assessment as mandated by SOX standard 404.

There are similarities and differences between the traditional or non-SOX audits and SOX audits. There are kickoff meetings, requests for documentation, interviews, findings, status meetings, audit recommendations, and a final report in both environments. However, SOX auditors vary from non—SOX auditors in expecting corporate executives to assess their control posture as being effective *before* a SOX audit begins; in using the control framework and control activities described by their client; in focusing on financial applications or transactions in applications that effect financial statements; in covering an entire audit period during the fiscal year to ensure reliability and sustainability; and in generating an attestation report, if possible. Attestation will only be possible if the controls are there and are working to the auditor's satisfaction. Unlike traditional audits, where management will get credit for having action plans in place to address issues, during a SOX audit all controls need be implemented and effectively working without any evidence of significant deficiencies or material weaknesses.

Chapter Ten

Development/Maintenance Methodology and Project Management

"Any activity becomes creative when the doer cares about doing it right, or doing it better."

—John Updike

Introduction

When auditors conduct an audit, they are interested in understanding the methodology applied by an application development organization, and in assessing the effectiveness of how the methodology is being managed. There is a good chance that they will query the auditee about the software methodology, processes and tools used to deliver work products for all efforts, regardless of size, urgency, or complexity. This will include projects, maintenance efforts, enhancement work and emergencies. The auditors look for processes that have proven to be successful and evidence of effective execution with supporting control activities. Auditors could ask the following types of questions:

> ➢ How do your processes differ for various work efforts? For example, how do your processes for developing projects compare with processes for coding emergency changes?
> ➢ What documentation should exist for one work effort as opposed to another (e.g., owner pre-approval for projects versus post approvals for emergencies)?
> ➢ Are there different activities used for small work efforts versus large projects, since no one expects to see the same rigor applied to addressing a three line coding change as would be applied to a two year project?
> ➢ What are the deciding factors in categorizing work efforts (e.g., the size of the work effort measured in days or hours)?
> ➢ When is a high level design expected to be documented?
> ➢ When are regression test results expected?
> ➢ Should a technical design document be updated?
> ➢ When should peer reviews be conducted?
> ➢ Who is responsible to ensure that the methodology is being followed?

I have been involved in too many audits where expectations were not understood during the initial phase and as a consequence, the auditors wasted a significant number of hours attempting to audit something that just was not there, nor was expected to be. Why should they look for a project plan for a one hour change? It makes little or no sense. However, it does make sense for a six month project. The next logical question is where is the line of demarcation drawn that requires a project plan to be developed? It is somewhere between one hour and six months, but where? It is important to realize that when external auditors audit your company they will probably find that your processes and procedures will most likely differ to some degree from the processes and procedures found in other companies audited, even though the methodology you use may be the same. Therefore, setting and agreeing on expectations for your audit is extremely important, since the auditors could expect your definition of work efforts and processes to parallel those reviewed during a previous audit. Your auditor should know what he or she should expect to see as a result of their understanding your methodology.

The methodology at your company should address all application development and maintenance activities throughout work effort life cycles. In addition to reviewing methodology and processes, the auditors will probably be evaluating and passing judgment on performance measurements, quality controls, risk management, and tools used in support of the methodology.

When methodology is chosen for a project, it will be the responsibility of a *project manager* to manage the project and to deliver it on time, within an accepted quality level, using the selected methodology. The project manager is responsible for planning, organizing, monitoring, and controlling all aspects of the project through its various stages for all work efforts to meet or exceed customer expectations. This would include but not be limited to the following:

➢ Work Management (Project Plan)
➢ Testing Activities
➢ Metrics
➢ Quality Management
➢ Task Management
➢ Risk Management
➢ Production Change Management
➢ Tracking and Control work efforts (via project managers' control book)
➢ Obtaining Customer Sign-offs (I will talk more about this in Chapter Eleven where I discuss production change management).

If we look at emergencies or very small corrective maintenance code changes, there might be only one person responsible for the coding who might also act as, project manager. The same individual can perform two functions. The larger and more complex the work effort is, the more it is likely that the project manager will need to be another individual. In large projects the project manager's only responsibility might be to manage the project and he or she might not even do any coding. He or she will wear but one hat. A coder does the coding and a project manager manages

Project management is a highly regarded role in today's IT community and project management certification is an objective of many IT professionals. Project managers are sought after not only in application development organizations but in IT operational organizations as well—anywhere projects need to be effectively managed to ensure success. For example, opening a new data center, switching over to a new operating system, or transitioning to new hardware requires large work efforts with extensive, well controlled projects that are established and managed by experienced project managers.

In this chapter there is a focus on development *methodology* used for various work efforts and the activities associated with *managing* them. Many of these activities are discussed again in Chapter Eleven: Production Change Management, but in there the attention is on control activities and the *validation* of execution.

SEI

When discussing methodology with external auditors, it would probably be to your advantage to make them aware if you are using Software Engineering Institute (SEI) methodology and discuss your maturity level. However, using SEI methodology will only open the door that could lead to attestation of control effectiveness by the auditors. You will still need to demonstrate effective execution of the methodology being followed. Background information on SEI might be helpful.

In response to a perceived crisis in software development related to escalating software cost and quality problems, the Department of Defense established the Software Engineering Institute (SEI) at Carnegie Mellon University in Pittsburg Pennsylvania in 1984 and established a federally funded research and development center (FFRDC). In 1988 SEI began the development of a process improvement model for software engineering. In August 1991, the first version of the Capability Maturity Model for Software (SW-CMM) was published by the SEI. A Capability Maturity Model (CMM) is a reference model of mature practices in a specified discipline, used to improve and appraise a group's capability to perform that discipline.

CMM has five maturity levels by which a company is rated. The rating given by SEI is a formal certification; you are certified at a maturity level. The maturity levels are a predefined roadmap based on proven grouping and organizational relationships. CMM has eighteen Key Process Areas (KPAs) within the five maturity levels that are assessed. The eighteen KPAs range from maturity levels two through five (maturity level one is the ground floor and starting point). The CMM KPAs assigned to maturity levels two through five that a company is rated at are:

➢ Maturity Level Two
   1. Requirements Management
   2. Software Project Planning
   3. Software Project Tracking and Oversight
   4. Software Subcontract Management
   5. Software Quality Assurance
   6. Software Configuration Management
➢ Maturity Level Three
   1. Organization Process Focus
   2. Organization Process Definition

   3. Training Program
   4. Software Product Engineering
   5. Peer Reviews
   6. Integrated Software Management
   7. Intergroup Coordination
➤ Maturity Level Four
   1. Quantitative Process Management
   2. Software Quality Management
➤ Maturity Level Five
   1. Defect Prevention
   2. Technology Change Management
   3. Process Change Management

CMM evolved into Capability Maturity Model Integration (CMMI). CMMI raised the CMM bar. CMMI extended CMM benefits to the total project and organization and was a collaborative endeavor of over one hundred people from nearly thirty organizations that involved industry, government and the SEI. Its purpose was to improve best practices based on lessons learned and to provide a structural view of process improvement across an organization. Its intent was to encourage companies to set process improvement goals and priorities, and to provide guidance for quality processes and provide a vehicle for appraising current practices.

The expected benefits of CMMI are to increase focus and consistency in:

➤ Requirements development and management
➤ Systems design and development
➤ Systems integration
➤ Risk management
➤ Measurement and analysis

Similarly to CMM, CMMI has five maturity levels that corporations are certified at. They are:

➤ Level One—Initial
   Process unpredictable, poorly controlled and reactive
➤ Level Two—Managed
   Process characterized for projects and actions are often reactive
➤ Level Three—Defined
   Process characterized for the organization and are proactive
➤ Level Four—Quantitatively Managed
   Process measured and controlled
➤ Level Five—Optimizing
   Focus on continuous process improvement

CMMI has twenty-four process areas spread over maturity levels two through five depicted below. Please note that I have indicated which process areas are rooted in CMM.

- ➤ Maturity Level Two
    1. Requirements Management (in CMM)
    2. Project Planning (in CMM)
    3. Project Monitoring and Control (in CMM)
    4. Supplier Agreement Management (in CMM)
    5. Process and Product Quality Assurance (in CMM)
    6. Configuration Management (in CMM)
    7. Measurements and Analysis

- ➤ Maturity Level Three
    1. Organizational Process Focus (in CMM)
    2. Organizational Process Definition (in CMM)
    3. Organizational Training (in CMM)
    4. Requirements Definition
    5. Technical Solution
    6. Product Integration
    7. Verification
    8. Validation
    9. Integrated Project Management (IPPD) (in CMM)
    10. Risk Management
    11. Integrated Teaming
    12. Organizational Environment for Integration
    13. Decision Analysis and Resolution

- ➤ Maturity Level Four
    1. Quantitative Project Management (in CMM)
    2. Organizational Process Performance (in CMM)

- ➤ Maturity Level Five
    1. Causal Analysis and Resolution (in CMM)
    2. Organizational Innovation and Deployment (in CMM)

If a company is at CMMI level three or CMM level three, external auditors will probably be impressed but this will not guarantee that they will stop auditing and reviewing your controls. Do not have an illusion and false sense of security just because you have been certified at a maturity level of three or higher. I have seen issues identified by auditors, some rather serious, even though an organization was evaluated at CMMI level three.

Work Management Methodology

When an external auditor is auditing for compliance they could request to see your work management methodology. They will want to know how projects, enhancements, maintenance, and emergencies are managed. They will be curious to see how you define and distinguish work efforts and the process that is followed for each of them. They will also test for adherence to these processes. They will attempt to accomplish this by sampling a number of different work efforts. These work efforts will cover a range from emergencies to projects. You probably do not follow the same process for a project as you do for a minor maintenance effort and, if that's true, the auditors will need to know how your processes differ for the various work efforts. The following definitions are examples of how work efforts can be defined, but you certainly can use your own definitions, which may be different.

> ➤ An "enhancement" is an addition, modification, or removal of functionality from an application. Enhancement can run the gamut from a minor enhancement of just a few hours of work, to a major enhancement where the work is measured in months, to a "project."
> ➤ A "project" is a large major enhancement effort estimated at three or more months or five hundred or more hours of effort.
> ➤ "Maintenance" is generally considered break-fix activity where minimum work effort is required to keep an application operating without any negative impact to its original functional scope. "Maintenance" activity can be divided into "corrective maintenance" and "emergency fixes."
> ➤ "Corrective maintenance" is usually a change to an application program to correct the functionality of an application. The application or program is still operational, but not operating as intended.
> ➤ An "emergency coding fix" to an application usually needs to be made when an application has aborted and production processing has come to an unexpected stop.

These definitions could easily vary from company to company and the auditors can live with that. Each company will most likely have established their own definitions and that is okay, as long as the auditors are made aware of *your* definitions and *your* processes. The salient point to remember is that you need to ensure that the methodology that you are using defines work efforts and the process activities that are followed. This detailed process should be documented and readily available for review.

An example of where process activities might vary according to work efforts is shown in the chart below.

Work Management

Process Activity	Emergency	Corrective Maintenance	Minor Enhancement	Major Enhancement	Project
Service Request	No, probably operations problem ticket	Yes	Yes	Yes	Yes
Business requirements	No	Yes	Yes	Yes	Yes
High level design	No	No	Yes	Yes	Yes
Detail or functional design	No	Probably not	Yes	Yes	Yes
Estimate	No	Yes	Yes	Yes	Yes
Coding	Yes	Yes	Yes	Yes	Yes
Independent peer review	No	Yes	No	Yes	Yes
Unit testing	Yes	Yes	Yes	Yes	Yes
Integration testing	No	Possibly	Possibly	Possibly	Yes
Regression testing	No	No	Possibly	Yes	Yes
System testing	No	Possibly	Possibly	Yes	Yes
User acceptance testing	No	Possibly	Possibly	Yes	Yes
Parallel testing	No	No	No	Possibly	Possibly
Pilot testing	No	No	No	Possibly	Possibly
Technical design document	No	No	Possibly	Yes	Yes
Project control book	No	Possibly	Possibly	Yes	Yes
Operational run book	No	No	No	Possibly	Yes
Users guide or users guide update	No	Possibly	Possibly	Possibly	Yes

I have seen situations when auditors walked in and asked where the independent peer review was for a one line change that took fifteen minutes to code. You can't just tell the auditor that it does not make sense for an independent peer review of the coding because of the limited work effort involved. They will want to see your methodology and process activities and understand the criteria used for determining if an independent peer review should or should not be conducted. I will define each of the above activities, giving you an idea of what an auditor might search for.

➢ Service request: An auditor usually looks for a service request or change request approved by the application owner for the work performed. This will be true for almost every coding change that is sampled. There are exceptions. There are sometimes blanket approvals for emergency changes where there is no time to obtain approval before the coding is done or there is a post approval obtained after the coding change is promoted. The service request process needs to be documented addressing how it applies to the various work efforts. I will discuss service request management in greater detail in the chapter devoted to production change management, where I discuss validation.

➢ Business requirements: Business requirements in many instances will be just a few sentences or paragraphs written on a service request for a minor enhancement or corrective maintenance, nothing more. However, in the case of a project, there will probably be a separate requirements document that can be voluminous. It is important that the auditor is educated on when to expect business requirements and the form that they can take.

➢ High level design: There is no time for a high level design document to be drawn up for an emergency fix where the urgency is on fixing a program bug and restoring the application to operation. All other work efforts will probably have a high level design.

➢ Detailed or functional design: The auditors will need to know when they should expect to see a detailed design or functional design. There might be little value in a detailed design for minor enhancements or maintenance activities that are less than five hours, certainly less value than would apply to a major enhancement or project. Again, your process documentation should be clear on what is to be expected and when.

➢ Estimate: Estimates on how many hours coding will take makes little sense for emergency fixes but will have greater significance and increased value with larger work efforts. The cost estimated for the work to be done should be known as early in the process as possible, so that business decisions can be made on whether expending the resource is cost justified and if the effort can be afforded.

- ➢ Coding: I have seen few instances of auditors actually reviewing coding, but if they want to they should be able to review the source code. An example of what the auditors have looked for has been comments in the source program that indicate when the last change was made and by whom, and a brief description of the change.
- ➢ Independent peer review: Independent peer reviews are expected by auditors for many of your work efforts. Independent peer reviews are a review of work products by someone other than the developer. The auditor will expect peer reviews unless your process indicates when they are not needed (e.g., emergencies, corrective maintenance). When independent peer reviews are conducted, there needs to be evidence that they took place. Usually the evidence is filed in a project control book with a project manager signing off.
- ➢ Unit testing: All work efforts should require unit testing before promotion to production.
- ➢ Integration testing: Integration testing is the testing of a stream of programs to see if they work together and if the output of one program is acceptable as input to the other. Sometimes a change may appear to work well enough within a single program. However if there is an interface to a second program, the interface may no longer work as it should. You should on various occasions conduct integration testing to make sure that the stream of programs still produces the desired results. Integration testing, as I mentioned above, is essential if an application is feeding a downstream application. There is a dependency on accurate data. If interfaces between applications are involved, you will most likely need to ensure successful integration testing. The decision to conduct integration testing is made by the development team but the application owner should be aware when integration testing is conducted. Integration testing is sometimes referred to as functional testing where all of the functions of the application are tested. I have been the recipient, on more than one occasion, of auditors' requests to demonstrate integration testing for service requests that were sampled. When the auditors were told that integration testing was not required they asked for the documented business decision to ensure that it was not overlooked.

    There probably would not be enough time for integration testing for an emergency fix. Other work efforts need to have a documented decision made based on whether there are interfaces between the applications being changed with other applications. Your methodology should state the criteria to be used to determine when integration testing is required and when it is not.
- ➢ Regression Testing: Regression testing is a validation that the program still works as it did before, outside of the parameters of the new change.

The development team needs to validate that the change that was made did not negatively effect the processing of the programs and application output. They should ensure that there is sufficient testing conducted to verify that there were no unexpected impacts and that what worked before still works. Although the new change works, you want to be assured that the coding was not detrimental to the accuracy of the processing that was accurate before. As with integration testing, the regression testing is usually decided on and executed by the development team with the application owner being notified. Regression testing is not necessary for emergency fixes but auditors generally want to see when it is required. Auditors again will need to see evidence of regression testing or the documented decision and the rationale for not requiring it.

➢ System testing: Once a change is made it might work well in a development environment where there are test libraries, test files, development test cases, and a test environment. The question is, how well will the change work and will it work in a production environment? The project manager will usually make a decision on whether system testing is required and he or she will notify the application owner. System testing is usually conducted by another group, independent of the development work, which can run the change through a systems test and production environment using production data. This is frequently completed in a production environment as opposed to a development environment since there might be differences between the two. The differences could cause problems to surface after the change is promoted to production. This could be the case even though there was no problem in the development environment. The need for system testing usually grows exponentially with the size of the work effort. The more complex the change, the larger the work effort, the greater the need to obtain a comfort level by running it in a production environment. Again, system testing needs to be defined in your methodology with a requirement that the rational for the decision to conduct or not conduct system testing be documented. This will serve as an audit trail when undergoing an internal or external audit.

➢ User Acceptance Testing: User acceptance testing is usually conducted by the application owner using test data that he or she created or that was designed and created in concert with the development organization. User acceptance testing (UAT) will give the owner a higher comfort level with the quality of the work and greater expectations of valid results to be used in an end user environment. It is a decision that is made by the application owner with the development organization being informed.

Your methodology should discuss the rationale for UAT and when it is to be conducted.

➢ Parallel testing: This is another form of testing where after a change is made a test stream of programs is run in parallel with a production run or runs. The aim here is to be assured that the mapping of results from the production run and test run can be explained and justified, assuring everyone of the accuracy of processing. I have rarely heard an auditor ask about parallel testing but that is not to say that parallel testing criteria should not be part of the documented methodology. I have been involved with large projects where we conducted parallel processing for one to three months to improve the odds of the quality of our work effort. We ran our job stream in parallel with the existing production job stream. We had to assure ourselves that our output and processing results mapped to the current production processing, where expected. If successful, parallel testing will give the auditors a higher degree of comfort level with your project. Again, parallel testing makes no sense for emergency changes nor corrective maintenance but it might make sense for other work efforts, especially major enhancements and projects. The decision to conduct parallel testing is made by the application owner and development team. A decision might be made to run a parallel test for one run or multiple runs or not to engage in parallel testing due to the nature and simplicity of the change. The test process in your methodology should address when parallel testing is to be considered, and it should be required that the rationale for having or not having parallel testing conducted be documented.

➢ Pilot Testing: Pilot testing is sometimes executed if the SR required a large project to be developed. All of the above testing may have been conducted, from unit testing through parallel testing. However, if an even higher level of comfort is required, there is another choice. The application owner can decide that he or she wants to run the new project for a period of time (e.g., three months) before signing off. The difference with parallel testing is that you are running both test and production together to compare outputs, whereas, in pilot testing you are not running in a test environment. You have cut the string and are in production mode only. During pilot testing, you retain all production data and can rerun production cycles if the pilot run is unsuccessful. You need to have backup and contingency plans for reruns if needed. This decision is usually made by the application owner. If pilot testing is decided to be conducted it will most likely be done for large enhancements or projects.

➢ Technical design document: Similar to integration/regression and system testing, auditors can look at your methodology to see the requirement for when a technical design document needs to be updated. The auditors will then probably need to see evidence that a business decision was made to either create a technical document or to update the existing technical documentation. Technical documentation may need to be updated for any change that affects the architecture or changes the technical design.

➢ Operational control book: An operational control book will be required when operations personnel need to know how to run the updated change. There may have been a new interface generated, in which case the operational run book should address the processing surrounding the new interface. Emergencies, corrective maintenance, and minor enhancements, most likely, will not require operational run books updates.

➢ User's guide: There may be a need to establish or update a user's guide if an application change results in either a new user table that needs to be maintained by an end user or new user reports produced. Again this would not be applicable for an emergency change and would probably not be necessary for corrective maintenance but, once again, the decision to create/update a users guide or not, should be documented and available to be shown to the auditors when requested.

➢ Project control book: Evidence of all process activities related to a large work effort should be found in a project manager's control book. The project manager should establish and maintain a control book that will guide him through managing a large project from beginning to end. This control book is a repository of all deliverables for the work effort. The project manager has responsibility for overseeing and delivering the work efforts and a control book is an excellent audit trail and tracking tool. For example, it would have business requirements, design documents and a project plan that defines all tasks that need to take place, with individual assignments, and target and actual completion dates. The tasks involve any action that needs to be performed by the development organization including obtaining requirements, coding, testing, and interfacing with the customer. The project plans would track each task until it is completed. If the control book does not contain the actual documents themselves, then pointers to the documents should be evident. If we refer to a maintenance and enhancement effort, the control book should still be readily available and under "High Level Design" it might say, "not needed." The important point is that there is documentation in the project manager's control book identifying what tasks need to be accomplished to support the particular work effort being addressed.

Each component within a project control book needs to be signed off or initialed by a project manager. This could be anything from receipt of business requirements to approving system testing to the rationale for not conducting a peer review.

Metrics

Metrics play an important role in an audit. Auditors will probably examine metrics that are generated and presented to both your executive management teams as well as to your customer. The auditors view metrics as another key activity. They will most likely ask for your documented processes that describe the metrics you are generating for your management team as well as metrics that you are generating for your customer. Not only can the auditors ask to see what metrics you are generating, but they can also request that they be shown a sample and evidence that they are being reviewed. Metrics without management review are useless. You should be ready not only to be able to show auditors that metrics exist but be able to show evidence that they were presented to and reviewed by the expected audience.

How do you demonstrate that the metrics were presented and reviewed? This can be done in notes or memos sent with attachments regarding the metrics, or in documented evidence of meetings. If notes or memos are used as documentation, you will need to show who they were sent to and evidence of receipt. If you present metrics in meetings you will need to demonstrate that the meetings were scheduled and took place, and provide a list of attendees. This can all be accomplished with meeting minutes. I suggest that all evidence of metrics being distributed and reviewed be retained for audit purposes and readily available. I have also seen audits where auditors were shown minutes of meetings that included an indication of the attendees but were not clear about what was discussed or where the subject was documented. Be careful to avoid these potential problems.

Metrics should measure the quality and timeliness of projects being delivered along with measurements indicating if they are being completed within established budgets. Metrics should be discussed with your management team and with your customer before establishing them. The same metrics may be used for both organizations. Examples of metrics that might be generated and used for either organization are:

> ➢ The number of service requests that were received in a given time period
> ➢ The number of service requests completed in a given time period
> ➢ Aging of open service requests
> ➢ Percentage of work efforts that had problems with testing, requirements, coding or installation

- The percentage of emergency changes turned around within a twenty-four/forty-eight hour window within a given time period
- Percentage of work efforts requiring rework in a given time period
- Average defect repair time
- Percentage of projects delivered on time
- Percentage of projects delivered within budget
- Percentage of service requests completed on schedule for maintenance and all enhancement work efforts
- Function point measurements
- Measurement of end user customer satisfaction
- Application availability
- The percentage of actual to planned budget used if budgets have been established for projects and enhancements

Quality Management

When auditors review your methodology they will probably inquire about quality management. We talked above about quality metrics, and everyone certainly wants to improve quality delivered in projects that they deliver—that's motherhood and apple pie—but the question is, how do you improve your odds of delivering high quality projects? How do you minimize the number of defects associated with the work product that is delivered? There are two quality reviews that I will address here; one is a systems assurance review and the other is the independent peer review that I mentioned earlier. The reviews that you incorporate into your processes supporting your methodology might have other names and you might even have additional elements but they should basically have the same objective: quality of deliverables needs to be assured.

System assurance reviews are examinations conducted by independent personnel who are not affiliated with the group directly involved with the work effort delivered. They are a separate group, usually residing within another department, who usually do not perform any coding. They review compliance to the methodology and focus on project management and the project control book. They would determine for instance if:

- Service requests were received and approved by the owner.
- Business requirements were generated.
- Test plans and results were completed.
- The application owner approved all test results.
- The owner application approved the promotion of code.
- Issues were documented and responded to quickly.

> There was adequate user education provided before the promotion of the project.
> Operational considerations were taken into consideration such as backup and recovery.
> Separations of duties existed.
> The health of the project was reviewed by management on a frequent basis.
> A project control book was established.
> The process for emergency promotion was adhered to.

The auditors will also most likely ask about independent peer reviews. They will expect peer reviews to be taking place throughout the development/ maintenance process. This is an example of a potential discussion between an auditor and auditee.

Auditor: "Do you conduct peer reviews?"

Auditee: "We have the customer review all of our testing."

Auditor: "That's not what I am looking for. What I want to know is, are there independent reviews by other personnel on the team who were not involved with the deliverable?"

Auditee: "We have peer reviews on the coding completed, on the tests conducted on design documents, and on technical documents."

Auditor: "Then if I sample a number of work efforts that relate to specific service requests, it would be safe to say that independent peer reviews took place."

Auditee: "Well. not exactly: it depends on the size of the project. If it was a minor maintenance effort, for example you may not see a peer review conducted on a design document, since it would not exist."

Auditor: "Then you have methodology that you follow and processes identifying where and when you have peer reviews?"

Auditee: "That's right."

Auditor: "Are the processes documented?"

Auditee: "Some are."

Auditor: "Okay, let me ask you if I can see the peer reviews that took place for the work efforts that I selected." (The auditor hands the auditee his samples.)

Auditee: "We do not document all peer reviews."

Auditor: 'Well, which ones are documented and which ones are not?"

Auditee: "That would be up to the individual department."

Auditor: "Then would I be correct in stating that there are no documented guidelines that state when a peer review should or should not take place and that the results need to be documented."

Auditee: "I'm afraid that you are right."

As you can see, in the above scenario the auditee is in trouble. Avoid the pitfalls that this auditee found himself engulfed in and ensure that your processes indicate when and where independent peer reviews are to be conducted. Independent peer review documentation or statements as to why they were not conducted for all work efforts should be evident in the project manager's control book.

Project Risk Management

There is always risk of a work effort not being completed on time, within budget, and with minimum defects. Project risk management is the process that addresses managing this risk, and the importance of the role played by project risk management usually grows exponentially with the size of the work effort. The larger the work effort, the more risk of failure and the more that can go wrong. Project managers are responsible for monitoring and controlling risk throughout the life cycle of the work effort, from requirements gathering to implementation. Major projects certainly have more risk than minor enhancements but there is almost always some risk, no matter how minute it may be. The project manager must address the following components of risk management as part of their responsibility:

- ➤ Identify and understand risks.
  (The risks can be identified by application owners or by development personnel.)
- ➤ Plan to contain the risk, eliminate it, or mitigate impact.
  (The project manager should establish and document a plan to contain the risk for the remainder of the project, eliminate it, or mitigate the risk with appropriate actions taken.)
- ➤ Monitor and communicate the risk to management on a regular basis.
  (The risk needs to be documented and brought to the attention of both development and owner management along with plans on how to address it.)
- ➤ Use the right tools for a solution.
  (The project manager must decide on the solution tool.)
- ➤ Reassess risk periodically.
  (Risks need to re-evaluated on a regular basis throughout the project as the risk may become greater or diminish depending on changes occurring.)
- ➤ Implement independent reviews.
  (Risks should be reviewed by independent personnel. Risk reviewers should be personnel who haven't developed a myopic view by being too close to the project, working on it every day.)

Examples of risks that could jeopardize the completion of a project or even minor enhancement are:

- ➢ Requirements are not being received in a timely fashion.
- ➢ Requirements keep changing and are never frozen.
- ➢ Requirements are not detailed enough and have to be redone.
- ➢ The project manager lost one third of his or her resources to another project.
- ➢ The software tools that the project is dependent upon are not working effectively.
- ➢ The owner does not have the resource available for user acceptance testing and midway through the project decides he needs help from the development organization in designing user acceptance test cases.
- ➢ Two key personnel who are working on the project are lost, one due to illness, the other leaving for another opportunity.
- ➢ The project manager's budget is cut during the project.
- ➢ There is a high dependency on the quality of input to be received from another application, which itself is scheduled to go live one month before your project and is in jeopardy of being late.
- ➢ The customer needs this project delivered a month earlier than originally targeted and there is no time for parallel testing.

The purpose of this list is to give you a flavor of the risks that need to be managed to have a successful delivery.

Summary

As part of an IT audit, you may be asked to describe the software methodology, processes, and tools that you have employed and will employ to ensure that all application/maintenance work efforts are delivered on time, with quality, and within allocated budgets. You should be ready, willing, and able to discuss your present methodology and supporting documented processes for all work efforts, regardless of size, with the auditors. You should have project managers managing the deliverables of each project. For large work efforts the project manager's responsibilities will be extensive and demanding. The project manager can utilize a control book to provide a tracking vehicle, a single repository of all deliverables, and an audit trail throughout the work effort's or project's life cycle. The project manager must manage compliance with the chosen methodology.

SEI CMM or CMMI certification at maturity level three or higher can be an indicator to an auditor that you have a well established methodology in place. However, they will still need to review your methodology processes and tools used, and validate effective execution, to attest to the adequacy of controls during the audit time period. Do not allow yourself the false impression that you will pass an audit just because you are effectively using an accepted and highly regarded methodology and all of its associated processes. You must be able to demonstrate effective execution of the control activity of your processes.

In addition, the auditors can express a desire and interest in reviewing methodology that you follow for projects, major and minor enhancements, and corrective maintenance and emergencies, and review your compliance. They can ask you what differences there are in the processes you follow for the various work efforts so that when they audit a sample of work efforts they will know what deliverables they should expect to see. They will probably want to review documentation that demonstrates that all of your processes are being adhered to. The methodology that the project manager is adhering to should address metrics that you are generating for your management team and for your customer. The methodology should also include quality management, testing activities, task assignments, project planning, and production change management. The auditors will not only be reviewing your methodology but will most likely review the execution of your processes as well. And last but not least, they will be curious to understand how you manage risk throughout the life cycle of any work effort from receiving a request through production implementation. They can ask you to inform them, who is monitoring risk and how it is being managed to provide assurance that all deliverables satisfy or exceed customer's expectations.

The following questions are a reference guide addressing audit readiness concerning your methodology.

1. Do you have a documented methodology that you are following in your organization for development and maintenance activities?
2. Have you attained SEI CMM certification?
3. Have you obtained SEI CMMI certification?
4. Have all work efforts been defined and the definitions documented?
5. Does your methodology indicate what processes should be followed for all work efforts from emergencies to large projects?
6. Are project managers assigned to manage your projects?
7. Does the project manager monitor all project activities?
8. Are project control books used?
9. Are project plans and tasks assigned to each project?
10. Are tasks identified within each project plan?
11. Are the tasks assigned to individuals?
12. Is there a target start and end date for each task?
13. Do you have quality assurance teams?
14. Are peer reviews conducted for identified tasks?

15. Does the methodology address testing expectations for all work efforts?
16. Does the project manager evaluate risk throughout development cycles?
17. Are risks frequently reviewed during the project?
18. Are risks reviewed by independent parties?
19. Are plans documented to mitigate or eliminate risks?
20. Is there documentation describing expected metrics that are produced?
21. Does the documentation indicate when metrics are to be generated?
22. Have metrics been established for your organization and are they generated per a schedule?
23. Have metrics been established with your customer and are they generated per a schedule?
24. Is there documentation that addresses who is responsible to review metrics?
25. Is there evidence that metrics were presented and to whom?

Chapter Eleven

Production Change Management

"Technology is like fish. The longer it stays on the shelf, the less desirable it becomes."

—Andrew Heller, IBM

Introduction

Without change, products soon become obsolete and no longer desirable. Production change management is a staple for any audit. It is one of their primary areas of examination during most IT audits. Production change management is reviewed primarily with two objectives. The first objective is to determine if a formal process exists that provides adequate separation of duties and protection of production data. The second is to ensure that the application business owner is involved throughout the production change management process.

In order to satisfy these objectives, auditors will examine production change management and applicable controls. This chapter highlights work management again even though the previous chapter, "Development Methodology and Project Management," addressed this topic. However, in this chapter I expand on control activities and *validation* of the execution of controls as opposed to *methodology*, which was reviewed in the last chapter. This chapter on production change management examines various and sundry controls that auditors subject auditees to, from an initial service request until the change is promoted into production. These activities include but are not be limited to:

➢ Work Authorizations
➢ Testing Validation
➢ Issues Management
➢ Library Control Management
➢ Code Migration

It is important to realize that some of these activities are discussed in other chapters in this book but the same activities fulfill a different role when discussing production change management.

For example, I elaborate on separation of duties in Chapter Four, but in this chapter when I discuss separation of duties under code migration, I refer to controls surrounding programmer's access to production data and production libraries. I talk about different work efforts in the previous chapter, discussing on a general level the different processes followed for different work efforts from emergencies to projects. In this chapter, I hone in on the testing conducted for these various work efforts and validation of testing results. I previously talked about quality and metrics when I talked about ADM methodology. However, change management controls help improve quality of deliverables.

In addition, there are metrics that are directly related to controls demonstrating successful change management (e.g., measuring successful implementation and percentage of rework activity). A well controlled change management environment improves the quality of deliverables and should reduce rework and improve overall success percentages that are being reflected in measurements reported.

Work Authorizations

Application changes start with a request for a work effort. This can be called a change request (CR), a service request (SR), a program change request (PCR) or any other terminology, decided on, by your company. I will use the term SR but you can substitute any other term that your company uses to perform the same function.

The SR is a request for enhancement or maintenance work and should be generated for almost all work efforts. Emergency changes are an exception where an SR may not always be required. However, even though there may not be an SR, the request for a work effort should still be documented (e.g., an operations ticket if the application aborted) with the necessity for a coding change, if required, being explained. Auditors will want to validate the existence of an SR for work efforts they sample or choose to review. If there was no SR, they need to examine the documentation as to why the change was made (e.g., emergency change). In most companies, the SR can be initiated by an application owner, developer, end user, or anyone who recognizes the business need for a change. If the work effort is not an emergency, the SR should have a documented process with a form that is required to be completed for authorization of the work to be done. *Auditors will focus on two controls, evidence of the SR and its approval by an authorized individual.* SRs need to be retained for the period of time stated within your company's process.

I have been a witness to the following scenario on numerous occasions and your manager being audited should not be surprised if he or she is subjected to the same. The auditor requests to sample a number of SRs. Your manager is able to retrieve the SRs and has them ready for the auditor's review. When the auditor looks at the SR, he or she asks who authorized the work that had to be done. Your manager tells the auditor that the process necessitates that all SRs be authorized by the application owner before work begins. The auditor has asked for ten sample SRs, a combination of various work efforts. They are distributed as follows:

1—Project
4—Corrective maintenance
3—Large enhancements
1—Emergency
1—Minor enhancement

One of the corrective maintenance SRs does not have an owner's signature and the auditor asks, why not? Your manager replies that it was approved verbally over the phone. The auditor looks at the process to see if verbal approval is accepted. The process states that approval needs to be obtained and the auditor wants to know how you can demonstrate that verbal approval was obtained. There is no audit trail.

The auditor makes a notation in his or her book and then looks at the other nine SRs and asks whose signature it was that appears on them. The auditor asks if your manager has a list of authorized approvers so the manager or his or her staff would know that the work was approved by an authorized individual. The manager supplies a list of owner management and key personnel who have been designated as owners. The authorized list includes all applications and an authorized approver for each one.

Five of the applications' SRs are signed with authorized names from the list, and four are signed by people not on the list. Your manager tells the auditor that there is a high turnover in the application owner's organization and that probably explains the four SRs in question. He or she recognizes two of the names as individuals who resigned last month, but does not recognize the other two. Your manager tells the auditor that they must be new individuals in the organization. The auditor asks for a letter from an executive or application owner designating the four approver(s) not on the list as authorized approvers and stating that the list needs to be updated. There is no such letter indicating that these four individuals are authorized approvers. Your manager says that he or she is sure it would not be a problem to call the owner now and ask for a letter. The auditor says that it will not be necessary at this time and makes another notation in their log.

The auditor asks your manager to explain why one of the approval signatures is dated October 1 when work had been initiated on September 21, ten days before the approval on the request. Your manager explains to the auditor that the reason for the post approval was that the approver and developers thought that the approval manager had signed. There was verbal approval and the approval manager realized one week after work began that she had not signed off. The auditor makes another note in their log.

The auditor after sampling ten requests has written the following in his or her log:

> ➤ One service request was not signed and there was no evidence of approval before work commenced. The manager stated that there was verbal approval.
> ➤ Four SRS have no evidence of being approved by authorized approvers.
> ➤ One SR was post approved after work began.

And of course auditors use percentages whenever they can to summarize findings. The summary statement that the auditor shares with your manager reflecting what the auditor was planning to use in the final report reads "60%

of SRs sampled did not have evidence of authorized approvers before work commenced on the service requests."

Examples of instances of work that will not generate individual SRs are emergency changes, as I mentioned earlier, and another category that I will refer to as "blanket" SRs. Your organization might use different terminology. The concept of a blanket SR refers to work to be done without explicit owner approval for each and every change. An example of a blanket SR might be for code changes that are for repetitive requests. For example, suppose that every month a new A/R report needs to be generated with the only change in appearance being the name of the month. A blanket approval at the beginning of the year can be generated by the owner asking for a new report every month. A blanket approval would eliminate the need to generate an SR every month.

Once SRs (regular or blanket) have been approved, they should enter a queue. The application owner then needs to control the prioritization and sequencing of the SRs to be worked on. This will depend on the needs of the business. The auditor will attempt to verify that the work is being prioritized by the application owner and not the developer. The auditor will look for evidence of regular communication with the owner where the SR queue is discussed and determinations made as to which SR should be worked on next. This communication can take place via emails or status meetings. If meetings are held where the SRs are discussed, the auditor will look for meeting minutes to validate that the meetings took place, what was discussed, and who attended. In addition to decisions being made as to which SRs are next in the hopper, there should also be regular communication between the development organization and the owner to track the progress of the work being conducted. The auditor again will look for documentation to support the monitoring of progress.

I stated that SRs need to be *approved before work was initiated*. What can cause an individual not to approve an SR? After all, isn't there a business need and isn't that why SRs are generated in the first place? The most important thing to remember is that the approver is authorizing the work to be done and this decision is based primarily on how much the change will cost versus the necessity of change. If it's maintenance activity, there may not be a choice; if it is an enhancement, then there usually is more importance and significance placed on an estimate of the work effort. There should be an estimate on the SR of the number of hours or days it will take to complete the work. The approver can then make an educated decision to go or not to go depending on whether he or she feels that the effort and cost are justified. Realizing that estimating is not an exact science does not reduce the benefit of the estimate being as accurate as possible. The estimate can be made by a developer but should be approved by a project manager or development manager and then by the application owner. It is the application owner who makes the final decision. The auditor will look for an estimate of the work effort and then expect to see that the estimate is properly approved before work is started.

Before coding commences there is usually a high level design document where the business requirements are stated. In a minor enhancement these business requirements may not be in a separate design document, but indicated on the SR itself. For major enhancements or efforts classified as projects, there will probably be detail design specifications, or a functional design document. Requirements and design documents must be approved by the application owner who approved the service request.

Testing

I talked about testing under methodology and processes as they applied to the different work efforts for emergencies, enhancements, maintenance activity, and projects. When auditors review testing there are a number of points that are noteworthy and should be highlighted.

Once work on SRs has started and coding has begun, a test plan should be developed. Usually, the test plan is developed by the developer and his or her project manager and sometimes their team, depending on the size and complexity of the SR. For example, for a project that is a large work effort of three months or greater, according to your processes there should be a detailed test plan. There are times when test plans are established by the application owner or his or her staff and sometimes when the test plan is designed as a result of a joint effort by both the developer and owner.

Auditors will look for documented test plans and if they are not documented, they will want to know why not. If auditors review emergencies or minor maintenance work (e.g., a one line change) there may not be a test plan. But the auditor will still want to know why not. As an example, you may have a documented process that states that test plans are not required if changes are less than ten hours. If that is the case, the auditor will audit to that process.

What should this test plan consist of? First there needs to be a decision made as to extensiveness of the test plans. The components of each test plan are dependent upon the effort required to deliver a quality product. All coding changes will need unit testing but decisions need to be made, that can be reviewed by an auditor, as to whether the following types of testing are required for the change:

- ➢ Integration testing
- ➢ Regression Testing
- ➢ System Testing (Functional Testing)
- ➢ User Acceptance Testing
- ➢ Parallel Testing
- ➢ Pilot Testing

For each of the types of testing, I have my own definition, which was given in the previous chapter when I discussed methodology. The definitions might vary from those used in your company, but that is not a problem. The important consideration is that your processes define the types of testing used at your locations(s), and that there is a documented business decision on whether to engage or not to engage in specific types of testing. For example, on numerous occasions I have been asked by auditors to explain why a systems test was not conducted for samples selected for the audit. Sometimes the explanation was simple. It might have been a simple change to put a date on a single report and a systems test was not necessary. And sometimes the explanation was missing. Auditors usually look for a business decision and rationale for the reason why a system test was not performed, and that reason should be documented within the test plan. The test plan could be as short as a few lines or as long as a multi—page document. It is important that the auditors are aware of decisions made as to the testing that was decided. Test plan documents should be readily available for the auditor to review.

There is one more element of the test plan that will most likely be subjected to an audit. The auditors will look for *test cases*. They will look for evidence that test cases were designed and documented. Test cases should be retained and available to the auditors whenever test data is used. This would apply to unit testing, integration testing, regression testing, and parallel testing. The same or different test cases might be used for these forms of testing. Naturally, test cases will not be available when production data is used. This would be true when pilot testing is conducted. If the application owner is performing user acceptance testing (UAT), the auditor may or may not review the test cases. He or she is more likely to review the test cases if the development organization is creating the test data.

Test results, since they can be voluminous, are not usually retained and available for review by the auditor. What is or is not expected to be available should be decided at the kickoff meeting when the scope of the audit is discussed. What is most likely is that the auditors will look for evidence of who conducted the test, when it was conducted, what were the results, and who approved the test results. They will look for the application owner to have signed off after all testing was completed, indicating that the code was ready to be promoted to production libraries. The sign off by an "approved" application owner before migrating code to production is a fundamental staple to a successful audit.

Issues Management

Throughout all testing performed, from emergencies to projects, issues can surface. The auditors will attempt to attest to the fact that there is an adequate issues management process. They will want to first see, as they always do, whether you have a documented process for issues management. Issues need to be recorded and tracked. Does the process require you to document all issues and record them for review? Are issues flagged if they are open for an extended period of time? Are there target dates for remediation? Are they recorded as being closed after being adequately addressed? If test results need to be validated to ensure closure of the issues, who performs this validation?

Issues should be recorded from audits findings, self assessments, peer reviews, or any controls review. Not only do all issues need to be recorded and a corrective action plan documented but there needs to be an assigned individual responsible for the corrective action, with an indication of target date and actual completion dates. Open issues need to be evaluated as to the reasons why corrective action plans are late and escalation to management as needed. In this chapter we will focus in on the issues that arise during testing a program change.

In our scenario above, the auditors asked the auditees for issues that resulted from the testing of sampled SRs. In many of the SRs there were issues recorded but there was no evidence of sign off that the issues were resolved. The sign off should be by someone other than the person who performed the testing. There should be an independent approval of the results and of satisfactory closure.

For some of the SRs the auditors did not find any documentation that there were any issues. The auditees simply told the auditor that there were no issues. The auditor's reply was, how did they know that there were no issues or if there were issues that just were not recorded? They were looking for a definitive statement that said there were issues or that there were no issues with the testing that was conducted. I have been involved with many situations where auditors did not find any documentation that explicitly stated that there were no issues. You need to make sure that such documentation exists providing this evidence.

Library Control

Development libraries should be separated from production libraries. If a change is required where code needs to be changed, a developer should be required to request access to the development library to retrieve the code, make the change, and move it back into the development library. Auditors will look at source program code to see if there are comments as to what the last change was (a brief description), who made the change, and when it was made. Auditors consider that this is a manual control, and that a developer who is about to make a change by looking at the comment in the source code will know if the change has already been made and when.

In addition, the auditors will look for version control to provide an automated control that the proper version of the program was accessed, worked upon, updated, and made ready to be moved to production. Version control will help ensure that only one individual can be working on a change to the same program at the same time. It would be very confusing if two developers were working on the same program at the same time, and difficult to ensure that the correct version was promoted. Version control will also help in controlling and ensuring that the right configuration items are pulled together for the promotion and that there is a comfort level that the correct components are in place. This can include data tables, job control language, and other program modules that are needed in support of the promotion of the program currently being changed. All elements needed for satisfactory promotion must be current, available, and effectively packaged prior to promotion.

Code Migration

Auditors will spend a significant amount of their audit time on code migration: promotion of code to production libraries. It is helpful for IT managers and company executives to understand expectations in this area. The best way to guide you through this process is to take you through a case study.

Ron and Sue, your external auditors, arrive at your company to conduct an IT audit. They inform you that they are planning to focus on your "code promotion" or promotion to production process. They want to ensure and be able to attest to the adequacy of your process and the effective execution of your control activities when code is migrated from test libraries to production libraries. You call in your application development and maintenance director with her management team and introduce them to Ron and Sue who describe the scope of their audit. In order to understand your promotion process and its execution, they first ask the auditee managers for their documented process. They want to understand the process first. They want to know how code is promoted from your test libraries to production libraries within your mainframe and distributed environments.

The applications that are supported are mainframe, UNIX, Oracle, or Web applications. The auditors are told that in the mainframe environment there is a separate independent department with a team of librarians who move code from test to production. They are not developers. In the distributed environment the auditors are told that the development organization is responsible for promotions and that the actual promotions to production are performed by developers who are not involved in the coding of the change. They are not librarians; however, there are tight controls in place to ensure separation of duties.

The auditors first request a list of applications running in the mainframe environment along with a list of all applications running in the distributed environment. They proceed to sample ten applications from each environment.

The auditors request a list of all mainframe promotions in the last six months for the applications sampled and a list of all distributed promotions in the last six months for those applications in the sample. They select two changes for each of the twenty applications in total, resulting in a selection of forty changes. For these forty changes they require the following:

➢ The SR supporting each of the changes
➢ A screen shot from production showing the version and date of the program promoted
➢ An indication of who is authorized to approve the change for the application
➢ An indication of the individual who performed the promotion
➢ The authorized approval for each promotion
➢ A screen shot displaying the last version and date of each program that was changed in the test library

After reviewing the forty changes the auditors had the following questions:

➢ The individual who did the promotion for eleven of the SRs was a developer in each case and they wanted to know the reason.
➢ Five of the programs associated with the SRs had different dates in the test library then the production library. Three of the programs had later program versions and program change dates in the test library than in the production library and they wanted to know the reason.
➢ Two of the programs had later program versions in the production library than in the development library and they wanted an explanation.
➢ There was no evidence for fourteen of the SRs that they were approved by authorized individuals before promotion and they wanted to know why.
➢ Three of the changes had no SRs associated with the promotions and they wanted an explanation.

Your managers attempt to answer the questions with the following explanations:

➢ The eleven developers, who migrated code to production, were supporting UNIX applications. There is limited staff and they have access to production libraries.
➢ The three programs with later program dates and version numbers in the test library had not yet been approved to be moved to production: they were awaiting approval.

➤ The two programs with later version numbers in the production library were an indication that the changes had not been tested. They were emergency changes that occurred in the middle of the night. There was not enough time to test the changes in the test library since the test data could not be created fast enough, so they were tested in production.

➤ Five of the fourteen SRs had no approval signatures and that was an oversight.

➤ Nine of the fourteen SRs that were approved by individuals prior to promotion could not be found on the authorized list. They were approved by individuals who transferred to other jobs or left the company and had been replaced. They were authorized at the time of approval.

➤ The three SRS were emergencies and did not have SRs associated with the changes. There should have been some evidence of post approval.

Follow-up questions by the auditor's were:

➤ Since it was a common practice for UNIX developers to promote code, what secondary controls (either preventive or detective) were in place to address the exposure of the developers promoting their own code?

➤ For the two programs that required changes in the middle of the night, and were emergencies, was there a documented decision made by the application owner to bypass regular testing?

➤ Was there evidence of notification from the application owners that the nine approvers had changed jobs or left the company?

➤ Is there an indication that the three changes that were emergencies without SRs were emergencies and post approved?

And the audit process continued.
The auditee manager's responses were:

➤ Developers who promote code in the UNIX environment are not supposed to be the same individuals who did the coding. However there is no secondary control for an independent control to review the changes made to production to verify that they were authorized.

➤ For the two SRs that were emergencies in the middle of the night there was verbal concurrence but no written concurrence that it was okay to test in production.

➤ There was notification on only three of the nine from the owners that the approvers had changed.

> ➤ There was documented evidence that the two of the three SRs with post approvals were emergencies and had approvals after the changes were promoted in production.

As you can see, the auditors were not easily satisfied and they just kept digging and digging. As a result of their review of code promotion, findings were written up and appeared in the final audit report with a request that corrective action plans be developed.

This was a hypothetical case study but not far from reality as it is based on actual audits.

You should not assume that your secondary detective controls will be acceptable to your auditors. You should review your secondary process with the auditors as early as possible to see if they would be satisfied. Naturally, as I have indicated throughout this book, separation of duties should be established wherever possible as a preventive control, and then you would not have to be concerned with secondary detective controls for program promotion. The golden rule that should be adhered to, if possible, is that *developers should not be permitted to promote code to production libraries.* If this tenet is broken and developers' access to production is to be accepted, you will need to have the auditors agree to a required secondary control process.

Let's start with the premise that developers on certain occasions need to have access to production to be able to promote code. You have a distributed environment and do not have the luxury of affording a separate support group that will promote code and provide you with separation of duties, as you have in your mainframe environment. What steps can you take? First you reach an agreement with your application owner that he or she owns the IDs and passwords that will allow production access. If production needs to be accessed by developers to migrate code from development libraries to production libraries, the owner can distribute the temporary ID and password to the developer, but on an emergency basis only. This would be done if the owner thinks that code should be promoted after test results are validated. The owner controlling access would be notified once the code has been promoted and the password would be changed at that time. In this situation the owner is assured that he or she has authorized access and code promotion after ensuring that test results are valid. The developers are permitted to promote control to production without standard separation of duties but with a secondary control in place.

Now let's look at another scenario. If a developer needs frequent access and has numerous production promotions, more than one on a daily basis, it may not be practical to use the emergency ID process. The owner may not want to have to be bothered issuing an emergency ID and password because of the frequency of code migrations. In this situation where there is no emergency ID issued, you will need a secondary control to validate that the change was initiated and approved for promotion by the owner. But how would you know when a change was made? Unlike the situation where the owner knows that code has to be promoted and issues an emergency ID, the owner is unaware of when the code was moved to production. A secondary control could require a monthly listing of all code promotions within the last month. This listing has to have, as its origin, a system generated snapshot from production that displays the last time the program was moved to production, and the program version needs to be indicated. Working backwards, an independent party would first verify that there is a corresponding documented change request for each program version promoted. The independent reviewer would compare the program version level in production to the program version level in the test library and ensure that they were the same. The next step would be to inspect documentation where the owner approved the migration of code to production. Once validated, the independent reviewer would need to signoff on the results of his or her review. The starting point must be the production library and not the development library since the purpose of this control is to validate authorization of all code promoted. There is no interest in seeing what is sitting in the development test library if it was not promoted. There would be no exposure in this situation where it was not installed in a production environment. To improve your control and minimize your exposure, this review should be done more frequently than monthly. This might not be practical if the activity is too voluminous. This is where risk management plays a roll. There is a risk here and the secondary control process and frequency of review needs to be examined by your executives and they need to accept or reject the frequency of monthly reviews.

Summary

Change management is a crucial process within any audit. What is important is that the auditee can demonstrate that all work is approved by authorized individuals, that there is documentation throughout all phases of the change management process, and that there are documented business decisions and rationale as to why various testing is not conducted or if any of the accepted process steps are not being adhered to.

In addition there needs to be an effective issues management process to record and track all issues that occur during testing; library control in place to provide for separation of development from production libraries and to ensure version control; and code migration controls to validate that only authorized program changes are promoted.

Examples of key production change management questions that the auditee should be prepared to answer and to demonstrate effective execution to an auditor are:

1. Is there a formal process to control changes made to production?
2. Are all change requests authorized by the owners of the applications or their designees? (These owners should be business process owners, outside of the IT organization)
3. Is there a readily available list of authorized change request approvers?
4. Is the list current?
5. If authorization is delegated, is there documentation supporting this delegation?
6. Are separate libraries established for testing of changes, rather than commingling test data with production data?
7. Is version control used to ensure that the correct program version is always promoted to production?
8. Are programs documented with a description of changes made?
9. Is accountability for a program change assigned to specific individuals?
10. Are programs documented with a description of who made the change and when?
11. Do all production changes, including emergencies, adhere to a change control process?
12. Is there overall adequate separation of duties with regard to change management with limitations placed on programmers and library access?
13. Are programmers restricted from promoting code from development libraries to production libraries?
14. Do librarians move code from development libraries to production libraries?
15. Are these librarians restricted from writing code and placing it in development libraries?
16. Are temporary libraries used when emergency code changes are made and are overrides pointing to these libraries restricted to a specified time period or less?
17. Is there a process that requires post approval if pre-approval can not be obtained for emergency code changes?
18. If developers are not always restricted from promoting code to production libraries, then are secondary controls in place for independent review and sign-off?
19. Have risks associated with secondary controls been approved by your internal/external audit organizations?
20. Is there evidence that all issues that arise during all testing activities are documented and tracked until resolution?

21. Is there a documented process that states when test plans are to be documented?
22. Does documentation exist in the test plan for each change that states what level of testing (e.g., integration testing, system testing) needs to be performed for all changes, no matter how small?
23. Are all changes reviewed and approved by application owners prior to moving code to production?

Chapter Twelve

Application Controls

"To err is human—and to blame it on a computer is even more so."

—Robert Orden

Introduction

When an IT audit is conducted, it could affect both computer operations and application development departments within the IT organization. It is possible that the audit will focus just on application development personnel or just on computer operations personnel, but frequently it will include both organizations. Many of the processes that will be audited will be mutually exclusive and will fall under the auspices of one organization or the other, but there are processes where there is overlapping of responsibilities, effecting both organizations. As an example, when the auditors are reviewing application monitoring, responsibilities are usually split between the computer operations organization and the application development organization. Computer operations personnel might receive the initial indication that an application has aborted and they will need to follow their recovery processes that might involve notifying application development to take correction action.

There will be occasions when responsibilities may be nebulous and the auditors will not know who to talk to, but they really won't care, as long as they get their answers. Therefore, the two organizations will have to rely on each other for support and in providing answers to the auditors. It is critical that there is synergy, close communication and team effort between both organizations when responding to audit questions and requests that penetrate both organizations.

To complicate the audits even further with regard to responsibilities, there is a third group that I mentioned in earlier chapters that plays a key role. This is the business application owner, frequently referred to as just the application owner, whose role and responsibility plays a significant role in an audit, necessitating a fully integrated audit among IT personnel and non IT personnel. It is impossible for an IT audit to take place without the understanding, knowledge, and review of business environments and requirements that precipitate the design and execution of IT controls. This chapter will focus on application controls and the integration of the IT community with the non IT community (the business application owner), the latter playing a significant role not only in driving the business from an IT perspective, but in controlling business processes as well. The subsequent chapter will further discuss operational controls.

The business application owner will be a driving force across both IT organizations (application development and operations) and their control processes. The IT audit, to be truly effective, needs to be an integrated audit between the IT and business community. Auditors will attempt to validate that control activities are effectively designed and implemented, and are auditable. The auditors when conducting an IT audit will be examining numerous controls: some of them will have been designed by the application development organization, some by the operations organization and some by the business community or business application owner. The implementation of the majority of these controls will probably reside with the IT organization, even if they were requested by the business application owner, who will have primary control accountability in the eyes of the auditors. The chart below attempts to depict the relationship among the three organizations referenced above.

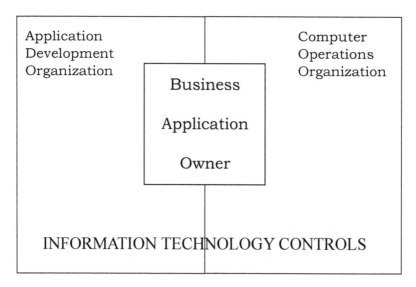

There are specific controls to be audited under the IT application audit umbrella. This list is not all-inclusive but includes the following strong candidates:

➤ Application Ownership
➤ Application Documentation
➤ Input Controls
➤ Output Controls
➤ Interface Controls
➤ Balancing/Reconciliation
➤ Processing Controls
➤ Application Access Controls
➤ Data Classification Controls
➤ Application Monitoring
➤ Application Backup/Recovery
➤ Service Level Agreements

In preparation for any IT audit your internal audit staff should examine applications and supporting control activities to ensure that the controls are effectively designed and installed, and are auditable.

The objectives of control design are pretty clear. Their purpose is to ensure that the processing of all data is:

> ➢ Complete
> ➢ Accurate
> ➢ Timely

and those assets are adequately protected.

The objectives of auditabilty should also be fairly obvious. Auditablity must address the:

> ➢ Verification of controls
> ➢ Traceability of results
> ➢ Documentation of controls

Application Ownership

Application ownership usually resides outside of the IT organization within the business community. Some companies have business process owners (BPOs) who own the business process (e.g., accounting) and then different business applications owners (BAOs) who own the applications within a particular business process. For example, we might have an accounts payables application owner, an accounts receivables application owner, an expense accounting application owner, etc.—all different, but all supporting the accounting business process owner. In some companies the business application owner and business process owner can be one and the same. For the purposes of this book, we will be looking at the business application owner's responsibilities.

Business application owners are the customers for whom applications are developed and installed. They are, in many instances, users of the applications themselves but in most instances they control and manage end user activity and application operation via effective application controls. The BAOs are involved with business strategies, establishing processes and objectives, and should play a significant role in requesting new application designs or in the design of enhancements to existing applications. The design, installation, and maintenance of these applications will directly support business processes. And for that reason, the applications must meet the ever-changing business environment. The BAO is usually involved with the day to day operations or in interfacing directly with the development departments.

In addition to the BAO having overall accountability for application controls as previously mentioned, there are many supporting roles that the BAO has responsibility for in relationship to the IT organization. The effective execution of these responsibilities, which will be addressed throughout this chapter, requires the synergy and close relationship of the BAO with application development organizations and computer operations organizations.

Application Documentation

When IT auditors arrive and ask for application documentation they may not be specific in the form of documentation that they are looking for. In a previous chapter I discussed process flows with control points as being identified and accepted as process documentation. If we take this one level lower, it would be helpful to have application flows for the applications supporting the processes. I have been the recipient of requests for application documentation that usually were satisfied by just narrative documentation (e.g., high level and detail designs documents, user's guides). However, there are many questions that will arise that could be more easily answered if there was an application flow at least depicting the application inputs and outputs and control points supporting the narrative. Application flows could be beneficial in navigating audit questions. Although application flow charts with inputs and outputs and controls are not essential for application documentation, they certainly would be helpful in identifying where control exposures exist and would make it easier to address most audit requests. Many external auditors today are looking for flows and control points on a process level as well as on an application level.

Auditors will want to know the functions that the application supports; its processing requirements; what its interfaces are, including all inputs and outputs; the operational schedule; where processing take place; the platform it is run on; the software used; identification of who promotes code; the promotion process that is followed; application security; identification of who monitors the application to ensure it is operationally effective; business metrics; libraries used for change control; actions taken for process rejects; the types of edits and audits that exist within the application; backups taken; application processing balancing that takes place, by whom and when; the number of end users and what data they access; application files and datasets that are generated and processed during a run cycle and their classification; etc.

There should be documentation that will help answer these questions as well as any other questions that might arise regarding application functions or controls, and provide a comfort level to the auditors that the application is well documented and responsibilities clearly understood.

Input Controls/Output Controls/Interface Controls

Input, output and interface controls are frequently reviewed by auditors during application control audits to ensure *completeness and timeliness* of processing. Auditors will want to make sure that there are effective controls to validate that all inputs received from sending applications and are transmitted to downstream applications are processed as scheduled. If a processing schedule calls for daily transmissions, how do you know that the right transmissions are received, that there is not a duplicate or that a transmission was not skipped? How do you know that all output that was supposed to be generated, was generated, and successfully passed to subsequent application for timely processing?

There should be a formal schedule as to when input is to be received from sending applications and when output is scheduled to be sent to downstream applications. In order to ensure completeness of processing, the sending application program needs to generate a header record on all files that contains a transmission number, date of transmission, record count, and dollar count. Each time the sending application program transmits a file they should be incrementing the transmission number. The receiving application program needs to verify the sequence number and add one to the last transmission received. If the transmission number received is one greater than the number expected, a transmission was probably *skipped* or if it is one less, a red flag should go up indicating a *duplicate transmission* is about to be processed. If the sequence number has been properly incremented and correctly indicates the next transmission, that is still no assurance that you received the right transmission. You could have received the same data if the sending application duplicated their processing with the same data although they ran another cycle. The additional control of checking and validating record counts and dollar amounts should raise the red flag of potential *duplicate data*. If you rely just on your balancing routines and just check record counts, that will not suffice, as there might be two consecutive transmissions with the same record counts. However, using the dollar counts as well as record counts, transmission dates, and sequence numbers should be helpful in avoiding duplicates from being processed. This is an excellent example of preventive controls.

Output control ensures that all output is generated that is scheduled to be generated and that it is distributed to the right organization. You should be generating a header record on all output that will be read and validated by the downstream receiving application. Your header record should have the same information, transmission number, date of transmission, record counts, and dollar counts. In this case your application becomes the sending application and the application that is receiving the transmission should balance to your output total. A schedule log should fulfill this requirement.

When you are undergoing an application audit, auditors will want to know what controls exist to ensure that all interfaces where received and successfully transmitted as scheduled. If you receive interfaces, there should be messages sent back to the sending application that the interface files were received and successfully processed. If you send interfaces to other application programs, you need to receive confirmation that they were successfully received.

This documentation should be retained so that an audit trail of successful confirmations can be demonstrated if and when asked.

Balancing/Reconciliation

There are times that external auditors will ask questions on processing balancing and/or data base reconciliation. You certainly need to be prepared for audits and from a business perspective, regardless of your audit concern, you need to ensure that you are executing effective balancing and reconciliation procedures. It is just good common sense.

When I refer to processing balancing, I am focusing on the balancing that takes place within an application to ensure integrity of processing. Balancing an application can sometimes be simple, but not always. The objective is to be able to demonstrate that all records were processed that were suppose to be processed, no more or no less. Balancing usually involves two items. One is a *record count* and the other is a *dollar count*. Both are used with one reinforcing the other, generating a greater level of comfort.

Let us look at an application that has 120,000 records with $1.3 million being inputted from an upstream application for a particular cycle. A control report that can be used for balancing should be generated at the end of the cycle. What would you expect to see on the balancing report? Would it show 120,000 records in and 120,000 records out to indicate that none have been erroneously dropped or added? Not that simple. There might have been 120,000 records in and 118,500 records outputted. Very possibly you could have 1,500 records rejected in this scenario or a combination of 1,000 records rejected and 500 records bypassed because criteria was not met for continued processing. In this case, your report should indicate 120,000 records read in, 1,000 rejected, 500 bypassed and 118,500 generated as output. Record input total should equal records rejected plus records bypassed plus output. Now, however, what if you had 122,000 output records? Could this be valid? Yes, this is a possibility; there could have been an explosion of records. Your process might require the additional generation of records under various conditions. The 2,000 additional records need to be explained. You need to show how many records were input, how many were rejected, how many were bypassed, and now how many were exploded, in addition to just showing the output total. As the permutations and combinations of processing scenarios increases, balancing will likely become more difficult. In any event, all variances need to be explained. The same would hold true for the $1.3 million processed. You may not have output records totaling $1.3 million, but all variances need to be explained and documented.

If you are updating databases during application processing, you will need to perform reconciliations to ensure integrity. The total of records started with should agree with the final record count from the previous processing cycle. You would then take into consideration records added and records subtracted to your number and that should reconcile to your closing record total. The closing number will then be recycled and become the starting number for the next cycle.

Processing Controls

We talked about timeliness and completeness of processing but we also need controls that will address *accuracy*. We need effective audits in place to check for valid data. We do not want to accept any data for processing that doesn't meet established criteria. We want to prevent erroneous or incomplete data from entering applications as soon as possible. When data is to be used for processing it should be edited for validity as soon as possible before being processed. It is important that rejected records appear on error reports generated to allow someone to work the errors for resubmission. As an example, if social security numbers are to be entered on all employee input records and if there are alpha characters, blanks, or eight digit social security numbers entered, these errors should be identified as soon as possible so that they can be rejected and resubmitted when corrected. Effective editing is an effective *preventive control*. Edits are important in every processing job or function. When data is used for whatever purpose it should be edited for validity as soon as possible before being processed.

Again, records that are rejected must appear on error reports to allow someone to work the errors for correction and resubmission. The auditor should look for error correction processes, controls to ensure that error records are recycled until corrected and aged so that there is control on how long they have been recycled. You will need to ensure that errors are worked on, corrected, and resubmitted for processing as soon as possible. As an auditor I found instances where rejected errors were not being worked. In one situation I found boxes of error messages that were being stored but not reviewed because the process for review was not documented and when the responsible party left the job rather abruptly, no one made any corrections and resubmissions. This was a billing application and resulted in a significant delay in revenue being billed. Timeliness objectiveness for working all error messages should be documented and corrective actions should be monitored. All uncorrected errors and rejects should be aged and reports generated that reflect these conditions, reviewed with executive management.

Backup & Restart Procedures

The auditor should determine if there are procedures to effectively back up and restore application data in case of application failure. They should also ascertain whether or not there are restart procedures to continue processing. This might involve taking checkpoints at various stages while the application is running for backup purposes. The restart or recovery procedures should ensure that no data would be lost, erroneously processed, or processed twice because of the failure. The failure may be the result of application processing flaws or hardware problems. It is important that the auditor ask for evidence, e.g., computer run logs, to see if the procedures were ever tested, how frequently they were tested, or were the restart procedures actually used during production cycles. If recovery was necessary, was it successful? How long did it take to recover and was all data restored? The auditor should also ask for a log of application failures and determine if the cause of application failures was known and what corrective action was taken.

Application Access Controls

Auditors will ask how access to applications is secured. This is an area where the application development organization needs to work closely with the operations organization. The auditors will ask who controls systems access to the mainframe or servers where the applications reside as well as application access and we do not want to appear paralyzed and unable to respond. The best approach is to describe how security is controlled on a system level and then on an application level and to provide the auditors with any documentation that is available. It will be advantageous at times to invite operations management and key personnel to meetings with the auditors when access controls are discussed to ensure an ability to demonstrate a smooth process flow and clearly defined responsibilities. You will need to solicit the involvement of operations personnel to discuss overall access control. I have been involved with numerous audits where this was of vital importance to auditors, yet many hours and days were wasted before the right personnel were present to help explain the total process. The auditors in many meetings with different personnel and after talking to many auditees realized that not all of the essential personnel were present who could answer their questions and had to extend additional invitations for numerous subsequent meetings after being given additional names.

It is important to realize that once systems are secured, we need to peel back the onion, look at another level of access, and ensure that applications are secured. *It is here that we address preventive controls, known as application access controls.* Individuals might need to have system access but another level of control should exist to see if they need to have authorizations to access application code, application data, tables, and libraries. Application access controls will focus on application owner responsibilities, the application access authorization process, and separation of duties.

Every application should have a business application owner who is responsible for the security of application data as well as the integrity, accuracy, and timeliness of application processing. The application owner will work closely with the information technology organization in executing their responsibilities. They are dependent on the IT organization to implement many of the controls that they deem necessary. Application owners can in many instances only request control measures that they feel that they need to be in place. It is incumbent on the IT organization to install such controls. Responsibilities of the application owner should include but are not limited to the following control functions:

➢ Determining who needs to have access to the application and communicating requests for granting access to the IT organization. This access can be granted to end users, developers, and other management and should be based on business need.

➢ The application owner should approve access and there should be a documented audit trail of such approval. This approval can be a form or note.

➢ The application owner also has the responsibility of notifying the IT organization of those individuals whose access needs to be removed with the lapse of a business need.

➢ The application owner should control the updates to any tables that are read and used by applications in granting access.

➢ The application owners should, at least annually, be asked to validate the continued business need for application access for each individual and be asked to document such approval. It is common to find instances where individuals who needed to access application data for business purposes were still on the access list even after they had left the department and no longer had a business need for access or left the company and in some instances had even died. Application owners had never bothered to revisit and revalidate the access list to their application after the initial determination.

The process of authorizing and granting access to applications is an extremely important deterrent control. We are not talking about system access, which is usually controlled by the operations organization as indicated above, but rather access to the applications running on a particular system where the application data can be of a sensitive nature. Many applications have built in logic or tables that add another level of access control beyond system access control. It is not necessary for everyone who has been granted access to a system to have access to each and every application running on that system. If procurement and payroll applications reside on the same system, it could be a breach in security for those individuals who have a business need to access the procurement application to also, by default, automatically have access to the payables application for which there is no business need.

The process usually starts with a request for access to the application and this access can be a view of data or a request to have authority to update the data. The request is initiated by the end user and should be signed by the end user's manager as well as the application owner as I indicated under the application owner responsibilities.

The auditor should ask, "Who controls userid authorization access to applications?" and "How is access controlled?" In some companies user ID authorization is controlled by the development or programming organization and in some situations it is controlled by an external group. It should not matter to the auditor who controls access provided that there is adequate separation of duties, which I will discuss later. What is important to the auditor is how well the process is controlled. Some of the questions an auditor might ask with regard to application access authorization are:

> Is there a formal documented process or request form used for requesting application access? (This form should be accessible to the end user or development personnel.)
> Does this process include approval by the requester's manager?
> Is application owner approval required?
> Does the request form indicate view or update capability?
> Does the form indicate the business need?
> Are request forms retained as an audit trail?
> Is there adequate separation of duties with regard to requesting, approving, and granting access?
> Is there a formal process for removing access?
> Is there an annual revalidation validating the need for those who have access?

Auditors, during an audit, will probably select a sample of applications that contain the most sensitive financial data and ask for a list of those individuals that have access. From this sample they will most likely ask for access requests and approvals for selected individuals. The auditors will review the date that the employees were granted access and validate that there still is a valid business need and when access was last validated (e.g., are they still working in the same department, are they still employed in the company?). Most audits that I have been involved with both from an auditee and an auditor's perspective have identified access exposures where individuals without a valid business need still have access. This is a result of a constant changing environment, movement of personnel to other departments and personnel leaving the business. Access lists are not reviewed daily and in many cases access administrators are not notified immediately of the need to remove access. A detective control is there to detect individuals who no longer have a business need but there is a gap from when one access report is generated and access need investigated and the generation of the next access report where an exposure exists. So at any time that an auditor arrives at a site and conducts an access audit there will probably be personnel who should have been removed but have not been because their need to still have access has not been determined. The most advisable action is to conduct a revalidation as soon as an audit is announced and to remove all personnel without a business need as soon as possible. The same will hold true for system access.

Data Classification Controls

During audits, I have rarely heard auditor questions regarding the classification of data, although it needs to be addressed when we are examining application controls. There are basic auditing questions that revolve around data classification controls in the review of application controls. Your internal auditors should at least ask the following questions and perform the following tests:

> Are documents properly classified? The auditor should sample a number of documents that he or she feels should be classified to see if in fact they are properly classified. These might include proposals for new work, payroll information, projected earnings etc. This exercise could result in some unexpected findings.
> Are there guidelines for the processing of confidential data and proprietary information?
> Do guidelines exist for electronically transmitting confidential data?
> Are there encryption guidelines that state when it is necessary to encrypt?
> Are there security precautions documented for mailing such information? The auditor should find out what these guidelines are, and if they exist, to determine their adequacy.
> What precautions are required when these documents are printed? Review areas where these confidential and/or proprietary documents are printed to see if they are in a secured office or area and not readily accessible to the unauthorized.
> Are there distribution guidelines for computer generated proprietary and confidential documents?
> Are there security guidelines for the destruction of classified information? The auditor should ask how the documents are discarded (e.g., shredders, confidential waste bins).

Application Monitoring

This is an area auditors can spend a significant amount of time reviewing and it can involve both the operations department and the development organization. The procedure for application monitoring should be documented. The procedure will need to address various questions such as: Who is monitoring the running of the application? Is it the operations staff, end user, developer, or all three? When there is an incident, where is it recorded? What types of incidents are recorded? Who decides if corrective action needs to be taken? Who is to conduct the corrective action? Where is the action recorded that resolved the problem? Let us look at a dialogue between an auditor and an auditee.

Auditor: Who is monitoring your applications to ensure that they are operational?

Auditee: Monitoring is done by the operations department for mainframe applications and by end users for distributed processing applications run on various servers spread throughout the country.

Auditor: Can you show me the documented procedure that discusses application monitoring?

Auditee: Sure.

Auditor: I see that it states here that incidents causing the application to abort are entered into a log by operations for follow-up resolution by the appropriate party. Who is the appropriate party?

Auditee: If it is an operational error, for example, a database can not be read, job control language problem, or insufficient space allocated, then the operations department will address the problem. If it is a program error, then development personnel will be notified for resolution.

Auditor: Is the resolution recorded?

Auditee: Yes, there is problem ticket entered into a log that is continuously updated from entry through resolution indicating who worked on the problem, when they worked on it, what action was taken, and the date that it was resolved.

Auditor: And if the application does not abort, is other monitoring performed?

Auditee: Yes. There are various error messages produced during the running of applications that require action to be taken.

Auditor: I would like to see these error messages for your accounts payable application. Can you generate a listing for the last six months?

Auditee: We don't keep the error messages for more than two months. The volume is prohibitive. The error messages for the last two months are contained in numerous boxes; do you want to see them all?

Auditor: Why are there so many? Is this application a problem?

Auditee: They are really not all error messages. Ninety percent are warning messages.

Auditor: What king of warnings?

Auditee: There is a message if space is a potential problem and then there is message for every interface received for totals generated.

Auditor: Just show me the error messages for the last week and indicate which messages you need to take action on based on your application monitoring procedures.

The next day:

Auditee: OK, here they are.

Auditor: This will do. Now demonstrate that if action was necessary, it was taken.

Auditee: I can show you that if there were error messages, they were initialed when resolved with a resolution date. This would include edit messages, duplicate record messages, etc.

Auditor: OK. But what about all the interface record totals? Do you have evidence that they were balanced?

Auditee: We resolve out of balance conditions but we don't keep records.

Auditor: Then there is no audit trail of action taken?

Auditee: That's right.

As you can see, there are many questions that can be asked when it comes to application monitoring. And the auditor can take two different approaches going in two different directions. The auditor can start with the error messages in error logs that indicate resolution to see the origin of the error, or he or she can start with an application's output for a selected day and see if the errors were resolved. Some auditors will take both approaches and call them a front-to-back and back-to-front audit.

Service Level Agreements

Application controls will frequently involve service level agreements. The auditor might ask what agreements have been documented that are used to measure the application's availability and performance. These are typically called service level agreements. They might involve the following:

➢ Application should be operational for a designated percentage of scheduled time (e.g., ninety-eight percent of the time).

➢ Critical errors need to be resolved within a specified number of hours (e.g., four hours).

➢ Number of outages during a period of time and total hours where the application is down should be agreed upon (e.g., less than three outages a month for less than one hour of down time).

➢ Number of errors generated as a result of code changes is a minimum agreed to number based upon the number of promotions (e.g., five percent of all promotions result in corrections).

Summary

When application controls are reviewed during an audit, it is essential to have the appropriate auditee present during the audit who is responsible for the application controls. This should be the application owner, who may or may not also be the business process owner. This is the individual who is responsible for deciding on the controls that need to be in place. He or she might rely heavily on IT (the application development organization and operations department) to help in the design of controls and certainly in the installation, but the ultimate responsibility lies with the application owner.

Application controls should focus on process flow and control points that will be examined by an auditor and revolve around ensuring accuracy and completeness of processing. These will include input controls, output controls, edits/audits, application monitoring, balancing/reconciliation, interface controls, backup/restart, application access controls, classification, and service level agreements. Following are questions pertaining to application controls that if used effectively can help you prepare for an audit.

1. Has an application owner been identified?
2. Are there process flows documented with control points identified?
3. Are there application process flows that identify inputs, outputs, and control points?
4. Are there balancing controls in place to ensure that all input received is completely processed?
5. Are there controls in place to avoid duplicate processing?
6. Are there controls in place to ensure that interfaces to output applications are able to process the data generated?
7. Are there detective controls to identify rejected errors that will ensure that all errors are corrected and reentered timely?
8. Are there adequate controls to ensure that application access is restricted to only those with a valid business need?

9. Is application access revalidated to ensure a continuous need for access?
10. Are backups taken and restart procedures in place in case of application aborts?
11. Are databases reconciled?
12. Are all outputs that are confidential or contain proprietary information adequately classified and protected?
13. Is application monitoring performed by either or both operational personnel and development personnel?
14. Are there procedures documented for application monitoring that address who is to conduct monitoring, how it is to be conducted, and when it is to be performed?
15. Are there error logs to demonstrate that application problems have been resolved in a timely fashion?

Chapter Thirteen

Operational Controls

"To err is human, but to really foul things up requires a computer."

—Farmer's Almanac

Introduction

As I mentioned earlier, when we talk about IT controls there is a strong dependency on the relationship and close cooperation between the operations and the application development organizations. When auditors are conducting an IT audit, they will be auditing areas that are under the total responsibility of the operations department (e.g., system password management), areas for which there are shared responsibilities between operations and development (e.g. application monitoring) and areas that are the responsibility entirely of the development organizations (application edits). This chapter will address controls that fall entirely under the purview of the operations organization. The controls that I will be addressing will be IT security controls, both logical and physical.

It is not my intent to duplicate volumes of security policies, instructions, standards, and guidelines that have been published and widely distributed. My objectives are to: 1) highlight and make the reader aware of areas that need additional attention and control. 2) stress the importance of having the right organizations and knowledgeable staffs in positions to effectively address IT controls, and 3) emphasize the necessity of synergy among the responsible organizations.

It is the role of the company's chief security officer (CSO) to establish an IT security department that will report to him or her, and be assigned the task of documenting company security policies and rules to be followed. The security department is also responsible for writing security instructions, guidelines, and standards and providing security education. It is the responsibility of the company's chief information officer (CIO) to have the technical systems programmers, application programmers, and operational staff design and install the necessary security controls supporting the security policies. It is the chief governance officer (CGO) whose responsibility it is to check and validate that the controls are adequately designed and effectively executed. And it is the combined effort of the CSO, CIO, and CGO to ensure that the security rules are being complied with.

The three organizations must work very closely together; this must be an effective, cohesive team effort. It is essential that the audit committee generate an atmosphere that promotes synergy among these three organizations whose goal should be to protect the company's assets and promote a controlled environment.

Most companies have IT security policies but they need to ensure that they are effective in protecting computers, networks, and information. Information technology services include networks, servers, workstations, host computers, application programs, web technologies, telephone systems, etc. Security policies are important to protect company information and systems from misuse and from unauthorized access from people inside and outside of the company.

Our vocabulary has changed significantly in the last twenty years, especially in the world of IT security. A new jargon has emerged with security terms that were non-existent or rarely used until recently, or if they did exist earlier, have taken on a whole different level of significance. We are in an new world of cyber space, the Internet, web services, the World Wide Web, e-mail, etc., and we need to protect this new world. It is vital that our corporate executives be familiar with the latest technology terms and that our internal auditors have sufficient knowledge to review applicable security controls in these challenging arenas. Examples of security terms that auditors should be familiar with are:

> Cookies: Small amounts of data shared between a World Wide server and user's browser that supplies information to the server about a user's identity and preferences.

> Encryption: The encoding of data as it travels through networks and the Internet. It requires the sender to encrypt and receiver to decrypt data using a special key.

> E-mail: Transmission of notes, messages and files from one computer to another.

> Digital Wrappers: Programs wrapped around another program or item such as an e-mail message. The wrappers act as gatekeepers to perform encryption, and secure e-mail or control the enclosed program from running under certain conditions.

> Firewalls: Hardware and/or software that protects networks from unwanted users gaining access.

> Cyber Security: A generic term used to define security in space as we send data over our networks.

> Internet Protocol Security: A suite of protocols used to secure private communications over the Internet.

> Intrusion Detection: The sensing of when a system or network is being used inappropriately or without authorization.

> Kerberos: A network authentication protocol that provides two computers with encryption keys for a secure communication session.

> Network sniffers: Diagnostic software applications that help monitor and identify performance problems.

> Secure Multipurpose Mail Extensions (S/MIME): An E-mail security protocol that prevents the interception and forgery of E-mail by using encryption and digital signatures.

> Secure Electronic Transactions: A standard for secure credit card transactions over the Internet.

➢ Secure Sockets Layers (SSL): A protocol that protects data routed between Web browsers and Web servers. Any web site address that starts with "http" has been SSL-enabled.

➢ Malicious Software: Software written to cause damage to or use up the resources of a target computer. Malicious software can be a virus, worm, or Trojan horse.

➢ Viruses: A set of instructions which when executed spreads to other, previously unaffected, programs or files. Viruses can do such things as display annoying messages, erase or contaminate files or alter stored data. They can even destroy a hard drive.

➢ Worms: Worms eat up computer memory and data as well.

➢ Trojan horses: Programs that appear legitimate but contain a second hidden function that may cause damage.

I will first discuss IT security roles and responsibilities. Once you have policy, guidelines, processes, and procedures developed by the CEOs and their organizations, you will need to develop and implement security controls and monitor their execution. I will be addressing logical controls, physical controls, and business continuity in more detail.

Security Responsibilities

There are numerous roles and responsibilities that need to be effectively acted upon for security to be effective within a company. Some of these responsibilities are:

➢ The CSO to set security policy.

➢ A security staff and IT security professionals to establish, design, implement and review security policy, instructions, guidelines, and standards.

➢ The CGO and the internal audit staff to review compliance to security policy, instructions, guidelines and standards.

➢ Administration management personnel monitor access to information.

➢ Data owners to determine the classification, sensitivity, and confidentiality of data and who has a business need to access it. The auditor should ask for and be given a list of data owners for key applications (e.g., payroll, accounts receivable).

➢ Process owner to ensure that their processes have adequate controls designed to prevent or detect fraud; unauthorized access to data; misuse, intentional or unintentional; or inappropriate distribution. The auditor should ask for and ensure that there is a list of process owners.

> Technical security experts to assist with the implementation of security controls and establishment of logical and physical controls.
> Company's employees to adhere to company security policies.
> Every manager to ensure that their employees are educated with regard to security policies, standards and guidelines.

Logical Controls

System Controls

System controls are preventive controls that address logical access such as password controls and levels of access, protection of systems from hackers, viruses, and unauthorized individuals. System access controls are our first level of defense against unauthorized access. Applications are installed to run on various and sundry systems and application access controls are another level of control supporting system controls. The objective of system level controls is to allow access to your systems only to those individuals who have a business need, restricting access to all others. When I refer to systems, I am talking about any system from mainframe to personal workstations where any application in installed and operational, used for the purpose of conducting business related functions.

There are individuals who are required to have system access. These individuals include but are not limited to:

> System administrators who establish the controls and manage system access.
> System support personnel who maintain systems.
> Programmers who design and maintain applications running on the system.
> End users who need system access to access the application data (application access controls are discussed separately).

When we talk about system access, we need to have:

> A procedure to address how users are granted access.
> A procedure that periodically reviews the business need for continued access.
> Procedures to identify and authenticate users.
> Procedures documented that define and classify resources to be protected.

There is a group of individuals who have system privileges, beyond system access, mainly systems support and system administration personnel, who are often regarded as having the keys to the kingdom. There needs to be tighter controls surrounding these privileged users because of their level of power. In a mainframe environment for example we are talking about those individuals who have system special, system auditor privileges and, in a UNIX environment, those with root authority. There needs to be procedures in place that:

➢ Grant privileged access when required.
➢ Review continued business need for privileged access on a regular basis. Revalidation should not be done semi-annually or annually as it should be for regular users, but more frequently, perhaps quarterly or monthly, since there is more risk involved.
➢ Remove access when no longer required.

Some examples of privileged users and their capabilities are:

➢ Users with SYSADM authority.
➢ Users with SYSCTRL authority.
➢ Users with SYSMAINT authority.
➢ RACF administrators.

SYSADM *authority* is the highest level of administrative authority. Users with SYSADM authority can run utilities, issue database and database manager commands, and access the data in any table in any database within the database manager instance. It provides the ability to control all database objects in the instance, including databases, tables, views, indexes, packages, schemas, servers, aliases, data types, functions, procedures, triggers, table spaces, database partition groups, buffer pools, and event monitors. SYSADM *authority* is assigned to the group specified by the *sysadm_group* configuration parameter. Membership in that group is controlled outside the database manager through the security facility used on your platform.

Only a user with SYSADM authority can perform the following functions:

➢ Migrate a database
➢ Change the database manager configuration file (including specifying the groups having SYSCTRL or SYSMAINT authority)
➢ Grant DBADM authority

SYSCTRL *authority* is the highest level of system control authority. This authority provides the ability to perform maintenance and utility operations against the database manager instance and its databases. These operations can affect system resources, but they do not allow direct access to data in the databases. SYSCTRL *authority* is assigned to the group specified by the *sysctrl_group* configuration parameter. If a group is specified, membership in that group is controlled outside the database manager through the security facility used on your platform.

Only a user with SYSCTRL *authority* or higher can do the following:

> Update a database, node, or distributed connection services (DCS) directory
> Force users off the system
> Create or drop a database
> Drop, create, or alter a table space
> Restore to a new database

Users with SYSCTRL *authority* also have the implicit privilege to connect to a database. SYSMAINT *authority* is the second level of system control authority. This authority provides the ability to perform maintenance and utility operations against the database manager instance and its databases. These operations can affect system resources, but they do not allow direct access to data in the databases. System maintenance authority is designed for users maintaining databases within a database manager instance that contains sensitive data. SYSMAINT *authority* is assigned to the group specified by the *sysmaint_group* configuration parameter. If a group is specified, membership in that group is controlled outside the database manager through the security facility used on your platform.

Only a user with SYSMAINT or higher system authority can do the following:

> Update database configuration files
> Back up a database or table space
> Restore to an existing database
> Perform a roll forward recovery
> Start or stop an instance
> Restore a table space
> Run a trace
> Take database system monitor snapshots of a database manager instance or its databases

A user with SYSMAINT or higher authority can do the following:

> Query the state of a table space
> Update log history files
> Quiesce a table space
> Reorganize a table

Last but not least is the *RACF (Resource Access Control Facility)* administrator. In a mainframe environment it is the RACF administrator who controls access to datasets. These are production datasets that should not be accessible to developers unless process or application owners have granted them access on an as needed basis. Anyone who needs access to a dataset in a mainframe environment should complete a request for authorization that is approved by the owner and granted by the RACF administrator. Auditors will review access lists to determine if access is still needed, or if it should have been removed. One of the most common findings of auditors is that individuals who had once been granted access based on valid business needs have since switched departments, or even worse left the company, and no longer have a business need—yet their access was never revoked.

Password Controls and User ID Controls

There are unique IDs that should be assigned to individuals who need system access. If they are system support personnel or end users, they should have a unique ID. This serves two purposes. First, it is a preventive control, which along with passwords should protect authorized access. And secondly, when the ID is unique, it will provide an audit trail of who has accessed the system or application residing on the system. System support personnel usually share user IDs to access systems, but this is the exception.

Passwords are one of the most effective forms of preventive controls that can be used. Coupled with user identifications, they should provide an added level of security. User identifications (user IDs) are usually static while passwords need to be changed frequently. Some of the questions that an auditor can ask with regard to password and user identification controls are:

➤ Have unique user IDs been established for system access?
➤ Are there guidelines that request that user IDs not be shared? (The exception here might be support personnel.)
➤ Is there a formal procedure to establish user IDs and passwords to gain system access?
➤ Does the procedure require management approval on a submitted request?
➤ Does the request form require business justification?
➤ Does the form state what system or systems access is requested?
➤ Is there at least an annual revalidation to review the continued business need to have access?
➤ Is there a process to revoke user IDs if they are inactive for a pre-established period of time (e.g., six months)? As an internal auditor, you should review instances where individuals have user IDs have transferred out of the department, left the company, or even died, but their access has not been revoked.

> ➤ Are there rules established for passwords regarding physical characteristics that will tighten control? These rules can address length and the use of numeric or alphabetic characters.
> ➤ Are there rules that require passwords to be changed frequently to enhance security?
> ➤ Are there systems controls that will check that passwords are changed to comply with the established security guidelines?
> ➤ Are there different rules for password change requirements based on job function? For example an end user may be required to change his or her password every six months while a privileged user such as a system administrator or operator may be required to change their passwords monthly.
> ➤ Are user IDs and passwords revoked automatically when there is a suspected compromise or when an individual no longer has a business need for access?
> ➤ Are there automated checks to see that passwords are not trivial? Extreme examples would be "1234567" or "passthru".
> ➤ Are levels of access established and assigned to user IDs based on business need? There should be decisions made as to whether individuals should have read, update, or delete authority, or any combination of those.

Viruses and Worms

A *computer virus* is a self-replicating computer program written to alter the way a computer operates, without the permission or knowledge of the user. Executive managers should understand the problems that viruses present as well as understanding what steps can be taken to protect systems from harmful code.

A *Trojan horse* is an impostor, that claims to be something desirable but, in fact, is malicious. Rather than insert code into existing files, a Trojan horse appears to do one thing (install a screen saver, or show a picture inside an e-mail, for example) when in fact it does something entirely different, and potentially destructive, such as erase files. Trojan horses can also open back doors so that computer hackers can gain access to passwords and other personal information stored on a computer. Although often referred to as such, Trojan horses are not viruses in the strict sense because they cannot replicate automatically. For a Trojan horse to spread, it must be invited onto a computer by the user opening an email attachment or downloading and running a file from the Internet, for example.

A *worm* is a piece of software that uses computer networks and security flaws to create copies of itself. A copy of the worm will scan the network for any other machine that has a specific security flaw. It replicates itself to the new machine using the security flaw, and then begins scanning and replicating anew. Worms are programs that replicate themselves from system to system without the use of a host file. This is in contrast to viruses, which requires the spreading of an infected host file. Although worms generally exist inside of other files, often Word or Excel documents, there is a difference between how worms and viruses use the host file. Usually the worm will release a document that already has the worm macro inside the document. The entire document will travel from computer to computer, so the entire document should be considered the worm.

Some viruses are programmed to damage the computer by damaging programs, deleting files, or reformatting the hard disk. Others are not designed to do any damage, but simply replicate themselves and make their presence known by presenting text, video, or audio messages. Even these benign viruses can create problems for the computer user. They typically take up computer memory used by legitimate programs. As a result, they often cause erratic behavior and can result in system crashes. In addition, many viruses are bug-ridden, and these bugs may lead to system crashes and data loss.

Virus detection is an important element of computer system security. Two resources available for virus detection are watchful users and watchful programs. Users should be cognizant of unusual or unexpected symptoms and utility programs should be installed to provide assistance.

Some signs that users should be watchful for and alerted to:

➢ Unexpected changes in the lengths of files
➢ Programs running longer than expected
➢ Programs taking longer to start than usual
➢ Unexplained decreases in amount of available memory
➢ Files vanishing
➢ Workstations mysteriously rebooting without reason
➢ Unusual displays or messages
➢ Any other unexpected program behavior

Programs should be installed that scan for specific characteristics or behavior of known viruses. These programs should signal the presence of many known viruses. As new viruses are identified, these anti virus programs are updated and the latest versions of these anti-virus programs should be installed on a regular basis.

Virus detection is one thing, but it is also very important to recover from virus infections. Recovery needs to address the replacement of every infected object in the system with an uninfected version and restore any other object that a virus may have damaged. Uninfected files could be restored from backups. It is important during restoring procedures to avoid re-introducing the virus into the system.

Questions that an auditor can ask are:

➤ Are users educated with regard to security threats and computer viruses?
➤ Are users informed of how to identify a virus, whom to call and what to do if they discover that they have been infected?
➤ Are backups kept of all critical data?
➤ Are backups maintained for all programs?
➤ Have recovery procedures been tested using backups?
➤ Where possible, have critical systems been isolated from sources of infection?
➤ Are programs that are added to a software library checked by authorized and knowledgeable personnel for possible infection?
➤ Are anti-virus software programs used to ensure that programs added to software libraries are virus free?
➤ Are programs that are vital to the business (e.g., accounts payable programs) tested on isolated systems before being moved into software libraries to see if they show any signs of infecting other programs?
➤ Are the latest anti-virus software versions used? (e.g., the latest version of McAffe or Norton)?
➤ Has a response team been established to quickly react to virus threats?
➤ Is there a procedure to remove viruses from infected systems once detected?
➤ Is there a procedure to isolate infected systems until they can be cleaned up to avoid infecting other systems?
➤ Is there a procedure for recording the characteristics of the virus and the steps to take to prevent its spreading, once it is identified, in case the same virus is detected again?
➤ Are anti-virus tools made available for easy access by any user of the company network?
➤ Are there security practices for network connections to outside organizations?
➤ Is electronic mail communication limited to non-executable files?

Protection of Systems from Hackers

In today's corporate environment, many networks are now connected to the Internet, which has enabled organizations to conduct new ways of doing business. These functions range from advertising products and services, to exchanging information and processing transactions over unsecured or inadequately secured network components.

We hear of more incidents each day of hackers entering our systems, and unfortunately they do not let us know when they will be intruding into our networks and gaining access to our web sites, systems, applications, and data. There have been numerous stories of hackers have entering into systems of large companies, obtaining proprietary information, and even diverting a company's money to their own accounts.

Some recent examples of theft:

> Three college fraternity buddies were able to penetrate horse track betting networks and learn the winners of various races before off-track windows were closed. They placed large bets and siphoned off more than three million dollars before they were caught.
> The Federal Trade Commission reported that computer hard drives containing more than 500,000 medical records of U.S military personnel and their families were stolen from a U.S defense department contractor.
> The FBI arrested a Russian who allegedly stole and distributed documents from the Internet describing Direct TV satellite television's service's anti-piracy technology. The documents were said to include details of the service's latest technology, controlling channels subscribers are able to access.
> According to the U.S. Postal Inspection Service, four suspects, including one former H&R Block employee, allegedly stole the personal information of twenty-seven H&R Block tax-preparation customers. The information was said to have been used to divert the customers' mail, open credit card accounts, and obtain tax refunds worth $8,000.

What is scary is the realization that these are just the stories that have been publicized. It is frightening to think of all of those incidents that are not reported, where the hackers have been elusive and have not been caught.

With the Internet being used more and more for financial transactions, and electronic payments being made using social security numbers, and more detailed individual security information becoming available, we are more vulnerable to hackers than ever before.

We are no longer just talking about mischievous and malicious viruses penetrating our systems by pranksters and technological pundits who are trying to outsmart the system, but about being vulnerable to theft and even cyber terrorism. The amount of damage, destruction, and financial impact that can be accomplished by professional hackers entering into our systems is beyond scary.

All that we can do is be prepared and take adequate measures to protect our systems from invasion and minimize their vulnerability. We have become more and more aware of the dangers of hackers who intrude into our systems and access confidential and proprietary information. We need to protect our networks. IT departments have become more sophisticated in developing and installing firewalls—preventing controls against unauthorized access—and in the installation of anti-virus software: detective and correcting controls. Firewalls are usually used to protect a network from the Internet, but they should also be used as a filter to regulate or gate traffic between networks on the company's Intranet.

What is a firewall? It is the first line of defense. Its intent is just like a door lock or security guard at the entrance to a corporate headquarters building. Its purpose is to keep unwanted people out of your network. The firewall functions as a filter or choke on the type of information that can be exchanged. The risk that we are faced with today is not limited just to access to a company's network at the office. As cable modems, satellite hookups, and other high-speed access to the home continue to become more popular, the risk of being attacked grows proportionally. A way to increase the level of security in your company is by using a firewall.

A firewall is a preventive control. Firewalls are software applications or hardware systems (routers) that enforce security and prevent inappropriate access to and between internal networks. Firewalls consist of rules that review each packet of data as it passes through the firewall. The rules can range from what is the source of data to what is the destination to the time of day the packet arrives. In simplistic terms, if the packet passes all the rules it is allowed to pass: otherwise it is turned away. All incoming requests for different network services such as file transfer protocol (FTP), and hypertext transfer protocol (HTTP) regardless of which host on the internal network will be the final destination must go through the firewall.

Firewalls are very technical and complex and few auditors will have the knowledge to perform an in-depth audit in this area. The IT auditors who will perform these audits must know how firewalls work if they are engaged in these audits. If the auditors do not possess the technical knowledge and skill, they must solicit help from subject matter experts (SMEs) to participate on the audit team.

To help ensure that the organization's firewall is protecting the company, the internal auditor or SME should ask the following:

➢ Does the company's Internet policy ensure adequate protection?
➢ Does the Internet policy permit any service unless it is explicitly denied?
➢ Does the Internet service deny service unless it is specifically limited?
➢ Is the firewall flexible in accommodating new services?
➢ Does the firewall contain advanced authentication measures, or and/or allow for the installation of advanced authentication measures?
➢ Does the firewall have filtering techniques to permit or deny services from specified host systems as needed?
➢ Does the firewall log traffic and suspicious activity?
➢ Are there procedures for reading and analyzing log results?

> ➤ Is there a procedure to update the firewall with software fixes?
> ➤ Does the firewall accommodate public access to the site so that public information servers can be protected by the firewall?
> ➤ Does the firewall language filter as many attributes as possible, including source and destination and inbound and outbound interfaces?
> ➤ Does the firewall use proxy services for services such as HTTP and FTP so that advanced authentication measures can be employed and centralized at the firewall?

A firewall is necessary and can prevent intrusion but it is no guarantee against intrusion. Keeping that in mind, it is important to realize that if a computer contains information that is top secret or classified, it should not be connected to a network, especially not connected to the Internet.

Auditors need to validate not only that there is effective anti-virus software that will recognize known viruses and correct their damage but also that there are adequate firewalls to protect systems, applications, and information from unauthorized access.

Physical Controls

Physical controls, such as badge readers and inventory control, will address access to restricted areas.

Physical access controls must be established wherever access by unauthorized individuals could result in disruptive or fraudulent activities with negative business effects. We will discuss building access, computer room access, tape library access and controls, printer room access, and access to financial areas.

Information Controls

Information controls will focus on classification and handling of proprietary information and protection against unauthorized access. When I talk about information controls I will be addressing two areas. The first is the securing of company employees' personal information and their right to privacy. The second is the protection of company proprietary or confidential information where the exposure of such information could be detrimental to effective company operations and revenue generation potential.

"Technology now permits millions of important and confidential conversations to occur through a vast system of electronic networks. These advances, however, raise significant privacy concerns. We are placed in the uncomfortable position of not knowing who might have access to our personal and business e-mails, our medical and financial records, or our cordless and cellular telephone conversations."—Chief Justice William Rehnquist

Personal Information

Chief Justice William H. Rehnquist sounded the alarm in the spring of 2001. The concern of the American public was focused on protection from invasion of privacy. This concern was significantly augmented by the events of 9/11. As a result of 9/11, courts are now endorsing the rights of government intrusion into the private records of Americans. There is now a growing belief that privacy interests can be sacrificed and are superseded by a compelling need to root out terrorists. There is also a large segment of our population that is of the conviction that privacy rights should be discarded when the detection of child pornography is an objective.

Privacy rights still should remain a prime focus in many situations where the protection of the American public is not the issue. The American people still have a right to privacy and protection of their personal interests from non-governmental agencies where the security of our country and safety of our citizens and their children is not an issue.

The internal audit organization should conduct audits to ensure that employee's privacy is respected. They need to ensure that neither managers nor fellow employees are divulging personal employee information such as personnel data, salary information, managerial evaluations, home telephone numbers and addresses, or any vehicle exploiting employee data for commercial use.

Proprietary and Confidential Information

The CSO should establish a security policy that addresses the classification of company information or data, who should classify the data, and how it should be handled, processed, distributed and finally disposed of. It then becomes the responsibility of the internal audit organization to ensure that the security policies regarding the protection of confidential or proprietary information are adhered to.

The following is a sample of questions that an auditor should ask with reference to information controls.

> ➤ Is there a documented security policy that addresses information controls? The auditor should ask for security guidelines and then review them for completeness.
> ➤ Are managers trained with regard to securing employee's proprietary information such as personnel information? Ask managers what precautions are taken with employee's personnel information.

- ➤ Is employee data and personnel information revealed only on a need to know basis?
- ➤ Are precautions taken to protect the employee's personal information at night or when the employee is not present?
- ➤ Are lockable desks, credenzas, cabinets and offices used to store employee's personal information, company confidential or proprietary information?
- ➤ Are there controls over the keys to these cabinets, credenzas, cabinets, and offices?
- ➤ If secretaries have keys to offices, desks and cabinets, are the keys secured? If secretaries have unsecured keys, the precautions taken by personnel to lock their offices and desks can give them a false sense of security.
- ➤ Are there security guidelines that discuss ownership of data? The auditor should sample information and data that he or she feels is of a proprietary nature and ascertain the owner's name. You will be surprised how many times you will not be able to identify an owner or it is believed that there are multiple owners without anyone really being held accountable.
- ➤ Are there guidelines for classifying data? Guidelines should state who is responsible to classify data and information and what is to be categorized as proprietary information.
- ➤ Are files and records that contain confidential or proprietary information and printed output properly labeled?
- ➤ Are there guidelines that caution against the use of phones, e-mail, and public conversations with regard to discussing classified information?
- ➤ Are documents properly documented? The auditor should sample a number of documents that he or she feels should be classified to see if in fact they are properly classified. These might include proposals for new work, payroll information, projected earnings, etc. This exercise could result in some unexpected findings.

Are there guidelines for the processing of confidential data and proprietary information?

- ➤ Do guidelines exist for electronically transmitting confidential data?
- ➤ Are there encryption guidelines that state when it is necessary to encrypt?
- ➤ Are there security precautions documented for mailing such information? The auditor should find out what these guidelines are, and if they exist, determine their adequacy.

➢ What precautions are required when these documents are printed? Review areas where these confidential and or proprietary documents are printed to see if they are in a secured office or area and not readily accessible to the unauthorized.

➢ Are there distribution guidelines for computer generated proprietary and confidential documents?

➢ Are there security guidelines for the destruction of classified information? The auditor should ask how the documents are discarded (e.g., shredders, confidential waste bins)

Building Access

Years ago physical access was limited to being requested to sign in at a desk in the main lobby or the issuance of employee badges. All employees were given badges that identified them as employees and they were required to present their badge upon request. Employees were later asked to display their employee badges at all times. When a visitor entered the building, he or she was requested to sign in at the desk and in most cases were given visitor badges and were escorted. All other entrances to the building were to be locked.

Two problems surfaced in the early 1980s at many sites. First, exit doors that could only be opened from the inside could be left ajar and accessible to unauthorized visitors. Second, in many complexes with multiple buildings, there were exit and entrance doors within the complex between interior buildings without security guards behind desks. Tailgating into buildings within these complexes was easily achieved.

The remedy that evolved, which is quite prevalent today, was the installation of badge readers that had to be used to gain entrance through every door into every building, the only exception being the main door to the main building where visitors could gain entrance and be requested to sign in. In some buildings today you cannot even leave a building, without using a badge to unlock a door. Auditors should check on the following:

➢ Does every door, with the exception of the door to the main building, require badge access?

➢ Are all visitors requested to sign in?

➢ Are visitors requested to indicate whom they wish to visit?

➢ Is a log maintained indicating what time visitors enter and when they leave?

➢ Are visitors required to be accompanied by an escort while they are visiting the premises?

➢ Are visitors given temporary visitor badges?

➢ Are these badges clearly indicated as visitor badges?

➢ Are employees displaying their badges? (The auditor should walk around to determine what is the norm is at the site.)
➢ Is there a policy requiring every employee to badge in and out and not tailgate?

Computer Room Access

Computing installations and supporting facilities must be administered as areas of restricted physical access when continued operation is considered essential or when classified information is on premise. I will talk about computer room access control first and then about tape library control, even though in many locations tape library control is a subset of computer room control since tape libraries reside within the computer room.

With regards to computer room control, the auditor should ensure that at a minimum the following control questions are answered:

➢ Is there a computer access list that identifies who should have access to the computer room? Individuals that should have access to the computer room are individuals whose primary responsibilities require routine access to the computer room.
➢ Is routine access limited and granted on the basis of verifiable and documented management approved business reasons?
➢ Is access to the computer room access protected with its own badge reader?
➢ Are unique badges supplied to those individuals who require routine access? These badges would be a special color, have a special tag, or indicate in writing that these individuals require computer access.
➢ Is there a visitor's log maintained requiring visitors to sign in and out of the computer room?
➢ Is the visitors log checked daily by a third person and initialed after being reviewed?
➢ Is there a procedure requiring visitors to be escorted at all times?
➢ Is there a procedure requiring that when a computer room door is to be left open that someone be present to prevent unauthorized access?
➢ Are all uncontrolled exit doors alarmed and clearly labeled?
➢ Are contractors who are admitted to the area supervised and monitored?
➢ Are master keys adequately controlled?

Tape library Access and Control

Tape libraries although frequently located within restricted computer rooms require even further access controls. Not every individual who works within a computer room needs access to the computer library. For example, computer operators might need access, but not necessarily contractors who are working on electrical problems.

Tapes used in business processes are assets and need to be adequately protected and tapes that contain classified data need to be protected even at a higher level. Access must be limited to fewer individuals than who even have access to the computer room. Each person with access to the tape library must have tape library responsibilities. The auditor needs to ensure that controls exist for tape library access and that tape assets are adequately controlled. Tape inventory controls are essential.

It is important to realize that all portable storage media must be inventoried and adequately controlled. Each tape must be uniquely identified and accounted for. There needs to be an individual responsible for taking inventory and to ensure adequate separation of duties, the inventory should be taken by more than one individual and reconciled by a manager. Physical tape inventory is an arduous job, but it must be done periodically, at least annually or when there is a large increase or decrease in tapes or movement to another site.

There are three procedures that a site must perform before an inventory control system can be considered to be complete and acceptable.

1. Maintain an inventory.
   ➤ Take the final inventory records from the previous inventory.
   ➤ Add to it all tapes added since.
   ➤ Subtract all tapes from this number that have been removed since the last inventory. This should result in the number of all tapes in your inventory.

2. Reconciliation to what is actually in the racks.
   ➤ Take the current system inventory status, which is what you think is in your physical inventory. This is your current status from your day to day record keeping.
   ➤ Physically compare your current inventory status to what is in your racks.
   ➤ Reconcile all differences and document the reconciliation.

3. Reconciliation of any differences between the two procedures.
   ➤ Both of these procedures should yield the same results. If they do not, reconcile all differences and document the reconciliation.
   ➤ The result is the current inventory that becomes the input to the next inventory.

Some of the questions that an auditor might ask in this area are:

➤ Is the tape library a separate room within the computer room?
➤ Is there an authorized list of those who have access to the tape library?

> ➢ Did management approve this list?
> ➢ Is this list current? (the auditor should sample names from this list and verify that these individuals still have a valid business need to have access). I remember performing audits in this area where individuals still having access, had retired years ago and the list was never reviewed to determine currency.
> ➢ Is there a process to control visitor access to the library indicating who entered and when they left?
> ➢ When was the last inventory taken?
> ➢ Was it reconciled to the previous inventory?
> ➢ If not, were all discrepancies explained?
> ➢ Who performed the inventory?
> ➢ Was there more than one individual involved in the inventory process?
> ➢ Were the inventory results reviewed by and signed off by a manager?
> *It is a common occurrence for managers not to sign off on reconciliations or if they do, they are not revalidating and it is just a rubber stamp.*

Printer Room Access

In many companies printers are located in separate rooms, accessible by all employees. The material being printed and picked up can be general business information or information of a classified nature. Questions that an auditor can ask are:

> ➢ Is the printer room locked?
> ➢ If it is locked, then who has access?
> ➢ Is it a key or combination lock?
> ➢ If it is a combination lock, how often is the combination changed?
> ➢ If it is not locked, is there a procedure for printed classified documents to be secured?
> ➢ If the room is not locked, are individuals required to pick up classified documents within a specified period?

The auditor as part of a physical security audit might want to walk over to printers that are accessible to anyone in the building to see if classified material is exposed. This would include employees as well as maintenance and contract personnel.

Financial area access

In addition to computer rooms and tape libraries, another restricted area requiring adequate control is the area where the financial department resides. This area should be restricted due to the confidentiality of many of the journals, ledgers, and financial information exposed. This area should be behind locked or card access doors.

There are other restricted areas that I have not specifically identified, such as legal department work locations and laboratories, which should not be forgotten. The controls in all of these areas are basically the same. Only authorized personnel with a business need should have access, either with a special badge or visitors should require an escort.

Business Continuity

What do we do if a disaster occurs? This question was never more daunting than after September 11th. Terrorist attacks, floods, hurricanes, power failures, fire, and earthquakes all make us realize that we need to address the reality of disaster and the challenge of business continuity. According to the *Internal Journal of Government Auditing*, the overall objective of producing and maintaining a business continuity plan is to "maintain the integrity of the organization's data together with an operational service and processing facilities and, if necessary, provide a temporary or restricted service until normal services can be resumed. Your businesses must be restored and operational after disasters strike. This entails people, systems, hardware, networks, telephone lines, and data."

Business continuity or disaster plans need to ensure that the critical business functions of the company are able to continue or restart in the event of unexpected circumstances with minimum disruption of service. Disaster plans must be developed that will address how to bring systems back up, how to restore data, what sites will be used, and where people will work. Not only do controls need to exist and a disaster plan documented, but it must also be kept current and tested to ensure that it is designed well.

Business continuity plans are developed by applications owners, operational management and key staff, and key personnel and management from all critical departments. Business continuity plans take time to develop and when completed should be signed off on and agreed to by all affected parties.

The audit committee must ensure not only that the company has adequate business continuity plans but that they have been tested. They should not only review plans but they should review test results. Business continuity plans need to be tested on a regular basis to ensure successful execution. At a minimum they should be tested annually. However, business continuity should be conducted more frequently if and when key locations and personnel change. Unfortunately, in many companies, business continuity is not a priority until a disaster hits; it is too late then.

Summary

This chapter discussed numerous operational controls under the subjects of roles and responsibilities, logical controls, physical controls, and business continuity. The topics covered under each of these areas were not meant to be all inclusive but hopefully they will give you a flavor of focus areas for audit readiness. Under logical controls the following topics were included:

> - System controls
> - Passwords
> - User IDs
> - Viruses and worms
> - Firewalls

Under physical controls the following were discussed:

> - Information controls
> - Proprietary and confidential data classification
> - Building access
> - Computer room access
> - Tape library access
> - Inventory control
> - Printer room access
> - Financial room access

In addition, this chapter touched briefly on the importance of business continuity plans.

Documented procedures are needed and good business judgment demonstrated to ensure that access to data and systems is adequately sufficient to *prevent* unauthorized access, and controls need to be adequate to *detect* misappropriate behavior. The operations departments have a major role in establishing and effectively executing processes and procedures that will accomplish the above but they need to perform their responsibilities in concert with the CGO, internal audit staffs, and application development organizations.

Chapter Fourteen

Spreadsheets

"Where is all the knowledge we lost with information?"

—T.S.Elliott

Introduction

When we talk about "integrated auditing" today and the interrelationships of IT and business processes, there are few better examples to choose from to demonstrate this dependency today in corporate America than the proliferation of spreadsheets.

Spreadsheets are being used more and more at an alarming rate throughout our corporations as a vehicle to manage businesses and to supply management with figures and data they need to effectively run their daily operations. It is not only spreadsheets associated with financial information but any spreadsheet manually prepared that drives a business decision. Imagine this scenario:

You have been asked by your manager to generate a report for the projected profit of the IT department over the next five years. You have the raw data available for projected revenue and expense for all nine IT departments for the next five years and assume that you can easily create a spreadsheet using Microsoft Excel. You can derive some simple formulas to calculate the profit and give your boss what she needs. You believe that you can do this in a day and she can pass it on to her boss as soon as possible and really make some points with her. You send it to her and take the next day off as a vacation day as you had scheduled.

When the report is reviewed by your boss the next day, she questions the numbers. It appears that the formula you used neglected to include the data for one key new application development department. She needs to change it but since you are gone and she is unable to get in touch with you, she asks Ray, another employee in your department, to adjust the formula and rerun the report. Ray can't get to the original data you used, since it was on your PC and under your password which no one knows. He has to derive the data from scratch. This takes most of the next day, but by ten o'clock that night, Ray has finished recalculating and sent it to your boss.

When you get to your office the next day your boss is furious and asks you and Ray to come to her office. She remarks that the figures for the new department are now there but she noticed that one of the computer operational department's profit numbers has changed. She asks how this happened and it is learned that Ray went back to the raw data and did not use the new profit numbers for the computer operation department that you had adjusted because you had received a note from the computer operations manager that there was a change in his numbers. There was no version control and Ray used the original numbers instead of the revised numbers. Your boss decides to schedule a department meeting and talk about controls surrounding the use of spreadsheets.

There are inherent risks associated with the use of spreadsheets that significantly challenge us in ensuring their accuracy and validity. These risks include, but are not limited to, incorrect calculations caused by invalid formulas; errors contributed to data entry and access restrictions to the spreadsheet data.

To quote Alyssa Martin from the December 2005 issue of *Internal Auditor*, "In August 2003, Jason Brown, the former vice president of finance for HealthSouth Corp., pleaded guilty to fraud and admitted he had prepared a false spreadsheet for auditors. Two months later, Fannie Mae, the largest U.S. financier of home mortgages, announced it had made a US $1.2 billion error in calculating its quarter earnings. A Fannie Mae statement attributed the error to honest mistakes made in a spreadsheet used in the implementation of a new accounting standard."

Spreadsheets allow designated personnel a host of individualized approaches for their design and execution. If the information tracked, logged, displayed, and distributed by spreadsheets were imbedded within well controlled applications, these risks would be diminished. Errors and discrepancies in spreadsheet results could be prevented/minimized if processing were integrated into these IT applications with access controls, logic controls, design and testing controls, etc. However, spreadsheet utilization and their associated risks are growing exponentially because it is thought to be cheaper and easier to put the processing in the hands of experienced spreadsheet users and to obtain the information needed to make business decisions much faster. Spreadsheets have user friendly features that allow individuals with varying degrees of computer proficiency to generate significant business data. It is a risk more and more corporations are willing to take. The purpose of this chapter is to weigh some of the risks associated with spreadsheets with the expense of adequate controls and to supply information so that business executives can make the right decision.

Background

As more and more individuals are becoming better educated and more sophisticated with their knowledge of Lotus 1-2-3 and Microsoft Excel, so has executive alacrity to have spreadsheets provide data to drive business decisions. The use of macros and multiple linked spreadsheets is becoming more apparent than ever before. There are few corporations where spreadsheet generation is not a daily occurrence. Spreadsheets users have increased significantly over the last few years and the need for tighter controls has never been greater.

Spreadsheet applications, or single programs, provide information used by management to make decisions which materially affect the operation or success of the business unit.

Simple calculations present the risk of misstatements. The use of spreadsheets and specifically the lack of controls over spreadsheets have become a contributing factor in reporting errors in numerous companies.

The statistics of spreadsheet errors is surprising. According to research by Raymond R. Panko, a professor at the University of Hawaii, *The Journal of Property Management* on July 1, 2003 stated, "30 to 90 percent of all spreadsheets suffer from at least one major user error. The range in error rates depends on the complexity of the spreadsheet being tested. In addition, none of the tests included spreadsheets with more than 200 line items where the probability of error approaches, 100 percent."

Potential Risks

There are numerous potential risks associated with spreadsheets that will vary depending on a number of factors.

The first thing that you must be aware of in evaluating the risk is that you understand what the spreadsheet is used for. As an example, is it used for personal use only or for making business decisions? Naturally there is minimal or no risk involved with a spreadsheet that is used for personal use (e.g., keeping track of an individual's expenses, an individual's appointments). Although this sounds simple, the risk even in this environment will vary and will be dependent. The risk will be greater, from a security perspective, if the appointments captured on the spreadsheet are for a CEO as opposed to a newly hired employee at the low end of the organization. One could be concerned with revealing information if a CEO's appointments indicated which customers he or she was scheduled to visit with in the foreseeable future or if a key executive's business travel destinations were known. Naturally, there is likely to be more of a risk if the spreadsheet is capturing business data and being used for making financial decisions. Examples of spreadsheets used where the risk would be significant, not only from a security aspect but in terms of integrity as well, might be revenue and resource projections.

Another risk could be the knowledge of the individual or individuals building the spreadsheet, performing testing, and verifying results. It is important that the individual who is inputting data and using formulas is well educated on the use of the tool being used, whether it be Microsoft or Lotus 1-2-3. How do we know that the formulas used in moving or calculating cell data are valid? The risk is greater the less knowledgeable the individual is who is preparing the spreadsheet and more risky if there is only one person responsible for collecting the data, processing the data, verifying the results, and distributing the final spreadsheet. You want separation of duties if possible and independent verification of spreadsheet numbers. This risk will of course be greater if the spreadsheet information is used in making critical business decisions.

Ask yourself how the spreadsheet is classified. If it is of a proprietary nature then it should be labeled as confidential and proper precaution should be taken in the distribution and dissemination of the spreadsheet information.

Another risk evolves around where the spreadsheet is stored and who has access to it. Again, if this is a one-person operation and the files associated with the spreadsheet are on a personal computer as opposed to a secured application data set, the risk is greater—because there is less control over spreadsheet access and data backup.

How often is the spreadsheet generated or updated and by whom? Is the spreadsheet generated daily, weekly, monthly, quarterly or annually? And once generated is it subject to be updated frequently? The risk will be greater the more frequently the spreadsheet is generated or updated. And who updates the spreadsheet? Is it just the owner or can any user update information? If multiple locations are then involved with multiple users being able to update the spreadsheet, what is the version control used to ensue that the correct version is being used?

There are inherent risks associated with spreadsheet data primarily in the areas of:

➢ Input errors with cut and paste mistakes, inaccurate references, or just careless data entry with rounding errors or incomplete data.
➢ Logic errors with wrong formulas or calculations being used.
➢ Spreadsheet layout errors with wrong cells, wrong headings, cell ranges, or functionality not meeting original specifications.

Proactive Measures

A number of proactive measures can be taken to reduce potential control issues with spreadsheet utilization. These are a few suggestions:

➢ **Take inventory of spreadsheets.**
The first pro-active step that should be taken is to take an inventory of who in the corporation is generating spreadsheets. Each spreadsheet should be inventoried with an owner identified, and a description of the purpose of the spreadsheet.

➢ **Identify all users.**
All users should be identified along with their access authority. Update authority should be limited to a minimum number of individuals (preferably just one person and a backup) with a necessity to generate the spreadsheet. Read access should be restricted to those with a business need.

➢ **Document desk procedures.**
Each owner should be required to document the desk procedure that is followed to generate the spreadsheet. This would include defining

where the input is coming from, detailing when and how the data is used including the formulas and external links, defining how it is stored, explaining how it is accessed, defining how it is backed up, and describing who uses the output and for what purpose.

➤ **Include spreadsheet generation in existing controlled application.** If possible, if the spreadsheet is significant to the business, the possibility should be explored to determine if the spreadsheet generation process can be incorporated into an already existing well controlled IT application that would enhance security and data integrity.

➤ **Ensure adequate separation of duties.**
As I alluded to before, whether or not the spreadsheet program or application can be used in an IT application within the infrastructure, separation of duties needs to be considered. You want to ensure that there is more than one individual involved in the process. You do not want one person generating the spreadsheet, having access to the spreadsheet and disseminating it for business purposes without at least another individual involved to independently verify the calculations and numbers being generated. The higher the business risk is if the data was not valid, the more thought should be given to establishing separation of duties throughout the process and to establish more independent reviews to validate the accuracy of the numbers. This would include having separate individuals reviewing test results and formulas used, and ensuring that data was not inappropriately changed or processed.

➤ **Validate all output.**
Testing is one of the most important steps requiring validation in the spreadsheet process due to the increased inherent risk of manual decisions and formulas used. Spreadsheet results need to be manually checked against the original data to reduce dependency on output derived from the formulas being used, since the formulas might be in error. Testing verification should be done on a frequent basis to ensure that processing is still valid and that formulas have not been erroneously changed.

➤ **Other controls that you should consider are:**
  ▪ A change management system should be used throughout the life cycle identifying and tracking changes to formulas and data, ensuring that all changes are appropriately authorized and that an audit trail is maintained for all changes including documentation changes.
  ▪ Apply standard software development methodology including gathering of requirements, design, testing, and library control.

- Utilize version control to ensure that the latest version is being used and that only one person can update the spreadsheet at a time in a controlled environment.

Generate a higher comfort level by having independent reviews of logic used and results verified. These independent reviews need to be documented and retained on file.

- Ensure that the spreadsheets are backed up on a regular basis and can easily be obtained if needed.
- Establish balancing and reconciliation procedures to ensure that all input is completely and accurately processed when data is obtained from other linked spreadsheets and all output totals can be accounted for.

Summary

Spreadsheets are one of the fastest growing vehicles used today to generate data and reports utilized by executives today in governing their business. The inherent risks are greater in this arena than in most other IT arenas because of the manual processing, the singular person autonomy over the accuracy in processing and security, and because of the recent emergence and adaptation of spreadsheets being catalytically responsible for driving businesses decisions. These factors coupled with the still needed utilization of standard IT controls and methodology makes this a critical control challenge. The following are questions that can be used to enhance spreadsheet control.

1. Has an inventory been taken to document whom in the organization is generating spreadsheets and for what purpose?
2. Is there an inventory taken at least annually and signed off on by management?
3. Has the spreadsheet technical platform and environment been identified?
4. Are appropriate security measures in place to prevent unauthorized access to the computer on which the spreadsheet is installed?
5. Is the spreadsheet, and source data used to create it, backed up?
6. Is the spreadsheet properly classified and is proper safeguarding established in distribution?
7. Is access to the spreadsheet adequately protected from unauthorized update?
8. Is read access granted to the spreadsheet on a business need basis?

9. Is the workstation where the spreadsheet is created and stored virus-protected?
10. Is access to the source code adequately protected?
11. Is the process for generating the spreadsheet adequately documented?
12. Are there backup personnel who can update the spreadsheet when needed?
13. Are all formulas and calculations adequately tested before production?
14. Is an independent review of testing performed?
15. Is an appropriate management review of the spreadsheet's testing results included in the procedures?
16. Do the desk procedures accurately describe, in detail, how the results produced tie to the source data?
17. Can the accuracy of the output of the spreadsheet be independently demonstrated?
18. Has the owner signed off on the delivered function having met the stated requirements?
19. Do the procedures contain a balancing and reconciliation methodology?
20. Is there a procedure in place that addresses who writes and approves requirements?
21. Has separation of duties been established to prevent conflicting access and duties for users of this spreadsheet?
22. Is there a change management process in place which includes documenting changes, testing, and an owner review of test results before changes are implemented?
23. If the spreadsheet is installed on multiple workstations, does the change process insure that the same version of the spreadsheet is installed on each workstation?
24. Were a test plan and test cases documented including expected results, actual results, who performed the test and when, problem closure, test acceptance and supporting evidence of results?
25. Was testing completed and/or validated by an individual other than (independent from) the developer?
26. Will a master copy of the final application be kept by an independent person to be used for periodic compares to ensure there are no unauthorized changes to the spreadsheet?

Chapter Fifteen

Outsourcing IT Controls (SAS70)

"When written in Chinese the word crisis is composed of two characters. One represents danger and the other represents opportunity."

—John Fitzgerald Kennedy

Introduction

You are the CEO of a large company and you have been asked by your board of directors for your thoughts on pursuing "outsourcing" the processes of your IT organization to an outside service organization or service provider. You have been examining ways to reduce expenses and increase profits and you bring your CFO into a preliminary meeting with you before meeting with the board. You realize that there will be considerable cost involved in outsourcing your IT operations but you hope that there will be long range savings and increased profits in allowing you to redirect your resources to focus on your core business. Additionally, you feel that by contracting with an outside service organization you will gain IT expertise and knowledge and have available the latest technology. Your CFO brings up a question that was not one that you previously asked yourself: he asks if the outsourcing service organization will be responsible for controls for processes outsourced to them, and if they will verify their internal controls as required by Sarbanes Oxley 302. He also asks, "How will you be able to verify their execution of their controls surrounding your business processes as required by Sarbanes Oxley 404, or will the service provider be responsible to validate effective execution?" He heard about a SAS70 report that could be a possible solution. The basic question is "When you outsource your IT organization or a part of it, who is responsible for the design of controls, and who is responsible for ensuring their effective execution and Sarbanes Oxley compliance?" A follow-up question is, "Where does the accountability stop and responsibility begin regarding Sarbanes Oxley?"

As the CEO you are accountable for SOX compliance for your company. You are the one, along with your CFO, who is required to sign off on your internal controls every quarter and annually certify that they are working effectively. When your company's auditing firm is auditing your company for SOX compliance, they do not care if you are outsourcing processes within your IT organization or not. They are commissioned to attest that you have certified all controls within your company's processes, wherever process and control responsibilities lie. You have ultimate accountability for the control posture of your company, but does your service organization have a responsibility to be able to demonstrate that their process controls are effective? The answer depends on what is written in your contract with your service provider. Contracts frequently state that a service provider needs to cooperate fully with the client company in satisfying all audit requests and allow external auditors to audit the processes and controls that have been outsourced to them. Service companies should be held responsible for the adequacy of their controls.

If you decide to outsource your IT operation, you will have a few choices regarding SOX compliance. Your options are dependent on the course of action agreed to with your company's outside auditors and with your service provider. One option is that your external auditors choose to audit both you and your service provider with regard to Sarbanes Oxley compliance. Your outside auditing firm can audit both companies to determine if the auditors can *attest* to the adequacy of controls for all of you processes, both those that you have kept and those that you have outsourced. This will require the auditors to perform 2 separate audits and they may want to avoid this.

As I mentioned above, your CFO has brought up an option to be considered, the generation of a service provider report referred to as a SAS70 report. In this scenario, your service provider uses their own outside auditing firm to perform a SOX compliance review. Their auditors generate a SAS70 report (explained below), and you can, if your external auditors are willing, accept the SAS70 report. Your external auditor will need to make a decision if they are willing to rely on a SAS70 report generated by the service provider's external auditors who *independently* audited your service provider's processes and controls. You will need to obtain concurrence from your external auditors that they will accept your service provider's SAS70 report.

Of course, if your service provider does not engage their own outside auditors to produce a SAS70 report, your choices will be limited and you will have to advise your service provider that they will possibly be subjected to a SOX audit by your external auditors.

SAS70 Background

*(The background information was obtained from **www.SAS70.com**, which is maintained and programmed by Scott Coolidge of Ernst & Young.)*

SAS70 (Statement on Auditing Standards No. 70, Service Organizations) is an internationally recognized auditing standard developed by the American Institute of Certified Public Accountants (AICPA). A SAS70 audit is widely recognized because it represents that a service organization has been through an in-depth audit of their control activities, which generally include controls over information technology and related processes. It is incumbent on service organizations, also referenced as service providers, to demonstrate that they have adequate control and safeguards when they host or process data belonging to their customers. In addition, Section 404 of the Sarbanes Oxley Act makes SAS70 audit reports even more important in reporting on effective internal controls at service organizations. One of the benefits of SAS70 reports is that it is an authoritative guidance that allows service providers to disclose their control activities and processes to their customers and their customer's auditors in a uniform reporting format. SAS70 provides guidance and insight to an independent auditor to issue an opinion of a service provider's description of controls through the SAS70 report, which will be discussed below.

Types of SAS70 Reports

There are two types of SAS70 reports:

- Type I Report—This reports on controls placed in operation as of a specified date (e.g., December 30, 2007).
- Type II Report—This reports on controls placed in operation as of a specified date and reports on tests of operating effectiveness during a specified time. This testing covers a minimum of a six month time period.

A service auditor (the auditor who is auditing the outsourced organization) has different responsibilities with regard to Type I and Type II engagements.

As a result of a Type I audit, the service provider auditor needs to express an opinion after:

- ➤ Determining whether the description of controls fairly presents the relevant aspects of the controls in operation as of the date of the report.
- ➤ Determining whether the controls are suitably designed to achieve the specified control objectives.

During a Type II audit, the auditor's responsibilities are the same as for a Type I audit, but in addition he or she needs to:

- ➤ Determine whether the controls that were tested were operating with sufficient effectiveness to provide reasonable, but not absolute, assurance that the control objectives were achieved during the period specified.

SAS70 Report Conclusion

An outside independent auditing firm will render its opinion on the control posture in its SAS70 report conclusion. There is no "pass" or "fail" conclusion as we are familiar with in traditional audits. The language of the opinion generally follows explicit guidelines as determined by the American Institute of Certified Public Accountants (AICPA). The opinions usually address four questions:

1. Did the service organization's description of controls present fairly, in all material respects, the relevant aspects of the service organization's controls that had been placed in operation as of a specified date?
2. Were the controls suitably designed to achieve the specified control objectives?
3. Were the service organization's controls placed in operation as of a specified date?
4. Were the controls that were tested operating with sufficient effectiveness to provide reasonable, but not absolute, assurance that the control objectives were achieved during the period specified?

The conclusion will either be a "qualified" report, in which case there were concerns that will prevent the auditing firm from rendering a favorable report, or an "unqualified" report, which is certainly more desirable. There should be no deficiencies or only very few non-repetitive minor issues or deficiencies for the opinion to be "unqualified." The deficiencies need to be significant or repetitive over the period audited for a qualified opinion to be rendered. The decision is a subjective one concluded by the service provider auditor.

Benefits of a SAS70 Report

A SAS70 report could benefit both the outsourcing company (client) and the service provider to whom the processes are outsourced to.

The client: A SAS70 report will provide the client with an independent assessment by an outside independent auditing firm of the controls within a service organization supplying you with outsourcing services. As I indicated earlier, the accountability for complying with Sarbanes Oxley rests with the CEO and CFO of each corporation. This is true whether operations are outsourced or not. The internal controls of the company being audited for SOX compliance could be in place and effectively executed, but there could be some significant control issues within the service organization that could prevent the CEO or CFO from certifying their *overall control posture*. And if your service organization's controls were certified by their management, there still might be some problems and difficulty with the outside auditors attesting to management's certification.

A SAS70 report without qualifications should provide a higher comfort level to the CEO and CFO as to the effectiveness of the service organization's controls and make their own certification easier, as well as making subsequent attestation by an their external auditors more likely. Client organizations that obtain a service auditor's report from their service organization receive valuable information detailing the design of the service organization's controls, a statement on the effectiveness of execution, and most important, an independent assessment by an outside auditing firm. The SAS70 report will be prepared by the service provider's auditors, and the client company's auditing firm should look favorably at approving the SAS70 report since the SAS70 is an accredited AICPA reporting process. Another advantage for the client company is that that they do not usually pay for the SAS70 audit, the service organization does. This is true if the SAS70 report is a "generic" report covering multiple clients that your service organization has, as opposed to a "specific" report for only the one client. If the SAS70 audit is not performed at the request of the service organization, then the client company would have to incur the costs for their external auditing firm to audit the service organization when a SOX audit is conducted.

The service provider: A SAS70 engagement allows a service organization to have its control policies and procedures evaluated and tested by the service provider's auditing firm, an independent, qualified party. A service organization can receive significant value from having a SAS70 audit performed by an independent auditor and a SAS70 audit report generated. A service auditor's unqualified opinion in a report issued by the independent auditing firm results in the service organization standing above its peers, demonstrating the establishment of effectively designed controls and execution. This could be an advantage and selling point when gaining recognition by their client, and in soliciting new business and trying to obtain additional outsourcing clients. On the other hand, if the report is a qualified report it will identify service organization shortcomings and will allow the service organization opportunities to make adjustments in areas that need improvement, potentially helping them to improve controls and contract new business.

SAS70 Process

When an outsourcing contract is signed it would be beneficial if both parties, the client company and the service provider, agree on whether or not a SAS70 report would be desirable by the client company and who would pay for the service providers' auditors to issue a SAS70 report. To help both parties reach an agreement, let us look closer at the SAS70 process.

As the CEO of a company engaged in outsourcing processes, you need to:

➢ First ascertain whether or not your company auditors will be interested in accepting a SAS70 report from your service provider's auditors to help them in their overall control attestation of the control assessments.

➢ If the contract requires that your service provider be responsible for establishing effective controls, you should validate that they agree that they will responsible for absorbing the costs of a SAS70 report by their auditors. This could depend on whether a "generic" or "specific" report is generated. Some service providers will pay for a "generic" report, but will ask the client to pay for a "specific" report.

➢ Ensure that your auditors will not audit your service provider for those controls that are uniquely identified in a SAS70 report but only those controls that have been excluded from the report.

➢ You will need to reach agreement with your service provider that the SAS70 report be unqualified for the report to even be considered by your auditors and your company.

As the service provider you will need to:

➢ Solicit your client company to determine their interest in a SAS70 report.

➢ Have your client company agree that your organization will not be subject to an additional audit by their auditors when they accept a SAS70 report that will demonstrates that:

▪ The service organization's description of controls in the report is presented fairly, in all material respects, and the relevant aspects of the service organization's controls have been placed in operation as of a specified date.

▪ The controls in the report were suitably designed to achieve the specified control objectives.

▪ The specified controls tested were operating with sufficient effectiveness to provide reasonable, but not absolute, assurance that the control objectives were achieved during the period specified.

➢ Absorb the expenses for your auditors to conduct a SAS70 audit (this could be restricted to a "generic" report).

➢ Conduct internal audits by your audit staff of your process controls with satisfactory conclusions before you invite your external auditors in to conduct a SAS70 audit.

➢ Contemplate having another independent external auditing firm helps you in preparing for a SAS70 audit by reviewing the design of controls.

➢ Evaluate whether or not you want to undergo the expense of having a SAS70 audit report generated. If your client has not indicated that they are interested in a SAS70 audit, you are taking a calculated risk, but much less of a risk than if they had definitively refused a SAS70 report. The latter situation would probably result in a waste of time and resources if you solicit the generation of a SAS70 report.

➢ Contact your external auditor to discuss the scope and schedule for a SAS70 audit if you have decided to pursue one.

➢ Decide with your external auditor to only include those controls in the SAS70 report that you believe will render an unqualified report, realizing that other controls could be subjected to your client's Sarbanes Oxley audit.

➢ Determine if effective execution of secondary controls will be accepted by your external auditors when there are exceptions to primary control execution.

➢ Contact your external auditors to begin the SAS70 audit.

➢ At the completion of the SAS70 audit, reach agreement with your external auditors on the issues and the determination of a qualified or unqualified opinion.

➢ Once an unqualified SAS70 has been generated, "generic" or "specific", then have your client review the report and indicate acceptance.

➢ If the report is a qualified report, then establish corrective actions to address exposures and have your external auditors return for another audit to achieve the objective of an unqualified report.

The service organizations controls, to be more readily accepted, should address five key controls that are COSO related and universally accepted by auditing firms. These components as I described in Chapter Two are:

1 Control Environment
2 Information and Communication
3 Control Activities
4 Monitoring
5 Risk Assessment

The Decision for a SAS70 report

Both the service provider and client face a difficult decision: whether to use or not to use a SAS70 report. This decision is not always easily arrived at, as there are numerous considerations.

First let us look at the service provider. There certainly are advantages of having a SAS70 audit conducted, as I mentioned earlier. You can gain significant respect and a foothold on your competition. An unqualified SAS70 report should put you in an enviable position of being able to tell your clients that you are a well controlled organization and have been individually assessed as having controls effectively designed and operating for a specified time by an independent external auditing firm.

However, how far should you go in soliciting agreement from your client that a SAS70 report will be beneficial, and do you take the risk of generating a SAS70 report, at additional expense, that might not even be looked at? This is tricky. You need to be sensitive to your client. Not only could you expose yourself to added expense for little or no benefit, but you might end up displeasing your client if you keep pushing them to accept a SAS70 report that they are not interested in. Be careful; use common sense. There is danger here as well as opportunity—see the John F. Kennedy quote at the beginning of this chapter—especially considering the possibility of receiving a qualified as opposed to an unqualified report.

Now let us look us look at it from the client's perspective. There are pros and cons in this scenario as well. The advantages of having your supplier of service conduct a SAS70 audit is that you can avoid additional expenses, since in order to have a successful SOX audit, the processes outsourced will need to be audited by your service organization's independent auditors or yours and it will reduce your expenses if your service provider incurs the cost. Another advantage is that if the SAS70 report is qualified and not accepted by your service providers auditors, your service provider will probably put action plans in place to have a follow-up unqualified report generated that will make them a better controlled organization, reducing the risk of control exposures to your company.

But as you would surmise, there are arguments against the client having their supplier of service generate a SAS70 report. The processes in your service supplier's SAS70 report, agreed upon by your service supplier and their external auditor, most likely did not have your input and may not map to your processes. In this case, the report will probably be unacceptable to your external auditor when they conduct a SOX audit. Another concern that you can be faced with is: what do you do if the processes and controls correlate to a large degree between your supplier of service and your company, but the controls are not complete? The processes and controls could represent just a subset of your processes that would be included in the report. For example, what if separation of duties is not discussed for thirty percent of applications outsourced, because for those applications promotion of code is done by your company and not the service provider? There would then have to be another audit conducted by your external auditors, regardless of the SAS70 audit, to get the big picture. Suppose your external auditing firm wants to audit all of your processes regardless whether they are being managed by your service supplier of you, and conduct their own SOX audit. You will have duplication of effort that you cannot afford. This is time consuming and will probably take your supplier of service personnel away from their dedicated tasks of supporting your applications and operations. There is no such thing as a non-disruptive audit and disruption will take place twice.

The service supplier and client company need to agree on whether a SAS70 audit is warranted and desirable. An independent Sarbanes Oxley audit by an outside auditing firm is mandated by legislation to attest to a corporation's assessment of their control effectiveness. However, a SAS70 audit is completely arbitrary and should be decided upon when it is in the best interests of all parties.

Timing of the SAS70 Audit

The ideal situation is to have the SAS70 audits in synch with the clients' service period. It could be a real problem if they are not. For example, if the SAS70 audit is performed annually at the end of May for a six month period and the client's fiscal period ends August 31, there would be a three month gap in the attestation of the service provider's internal controls. If the controls are not effectively working during this gap period, the attestation could be compromised, and fair game for the Securities and Exchange inquiry. Although expensive, one approach to address this problem is to have more frequent SAS70 audits. Some large companies request that SAS70 audits be performed on a quarterly basis to lessen the gap period.

Difference between a SAS70 Audit and a Traditional Audit

The major differences between a SAS70 audit and a traditional audit, some of which were previously addressed when discussing SOX audits, are:

➢ The service organization or client company requests a SAS70 audit at a specific time covering a specific time period. It is not mandatory. A traditional audit can be announced at any time but the auditee is usually told that they will be audited.

➢ The SAS70 audit needs to be conducted by external auditors other than the auditors conducting SOX audits, who can be the same external auditors who perform your traditional audits.

➢ The control objectives and control questions are discussed and agreed to between the auditee and auditor before the SAS70 audit is conducted. There should be absolutely no surprises during a SAS70 audit with regard to scope. The auditee is informing the auditor what the internal controls and policies are in his or her company and what controls were previously reviewed and certified by management. This is not the case in a traditional audit.

➢ SAS70 auditors will sample activity from the entire audit period. The controls need to be in place and executed for any sample selected during the audit time frame. The controls are either there and are being executed or not. There are no grey areas. If the audit period is twelve months, you need to demonstrate compliance during the entire twelve months. In a traditional audit you can get credit for action plans being in place or you can even avoid be cited for any issue if there was resolution prior to the audit commencing. A traditional audit is usually a reflection of the audit status at a specific time (the time of the audit) and does not look back to see if the issue previously existed.

➢ A traditional audit will be a pass or fail audit with a passing grade possible if, in the opinion of the auditor, major exposures are not found and control weaknesses have been identified by management prior to the audit and action plans are in place. A SAS70 audit is not a pass/fail but a qualified or unqualified report as to the ability of the external auditors to state whether controls are effectively designed and being executed for the time period for the scope of the audit, not if they plan to be.

Effect of SAS70 on Outsourcing

The jury is still out on the effect of SAS70 on Outsourcing.

With cost savings being a major objective of outsourcing, one compelling question is, "Does Sarbanes Oxley add to the cost of outsourcing, and will outsourcings become less popular as a result of Sarbanes Oxley, or will outsourcing ultimately reduce the cost of Sarbanes Oxley compliance?"

Other than the cost factor of achieving Sarbanes Oxley compliance via outsourcing, another crucial question in the equation is whether compliance will be more readily obtainable by outsourcing.

Stan Lepak, a vice president at Meta Group INC, believes that incompatibilities between SAS70 and Sarbanes Oxley will "dampen outsourcing, at least in the short run, until outsources can show that they have both the adequate controls in place and evidence to prove that."

Tom Eubanks, global leader for finance and accounting outsourcing with IBM Business Consulting Services, has a different view. "At first blush," he says, "one might think, why would you outsource in a world where Sarbox is in place . . . and the magnifying glass is on the finance function?" But Eubanks says that "companies are looking at outsourcing as a valid way to address some {Sarbanes Oxley} issues."

What we have then is apparently an opportunity for service organizations who have been the recipient of outsourced IT operations to demonstrate effective control postures. However, it is incumbent on service organizations if they want to expand their outsourcing offerings to be able to demonstrate to their prospective clients that they can help with SOX compliance via the generation of SAS70 reports. The cost of additional efforts might be higher than most corporations initially intend to spend on outsourcing, but the rewards are significant with the achievement of an outside auditor's attestation to effectiveness of controls.

Outsourcing should reduce the cost of complying with Sarbanes Oxley if service organizations are creative in how they facilitate the compliance effort and expand their opportunities for the future. It might be more costly for them initially to have their external auditors conduct SAS70 audits, but there should be opportunities for additional outsourcing contracts to be signed.

Summary

IT outsourcing is growing at an accelerated rate, but there are concerns now being raised by some corporations exploring outsourcing. These concerns focus on questions of Sarbanes Oxley compliance if IT processes are outsourced. Can corporations still sign off that they adequately assessed their IT controls if many IT processes have been outsourced? After all, CEOs and CFOs are still ultimately accountable for their corporation's controls, not the service provider to whom they have outsourced processes. Although service providers, via the contracts they sign, might have responsibility for the control effectiveness of the processes they execute, the overall SOX accountability remains with the client company. This accountability cannot be delegated.

An approach that is being taken today is service organizations having independent external auditing firms generate SAS70 reports. A SAS70 report (Statement on Auditing Standards No. 70, Service Organizations) is an internationally recognized auditing standard developed by the American Institute of Certified Public Accountants (AICPA). A SAS70 audit is widely recognized because it represents that a service organization has been through an in-depth audit of their control activities, which generally includes controls over information technology and related processes.

The Type II SAS70 report that is generally desirable, reports on controls placed in operation as of a specified date and reports on tests of operating effectiveness during a specified time. This testing covers a minimum of a six month period.

The benefit to a client who outsources their processes is that the service provider will usually pay for the expense of their outside auditors conducting a SAS70 audit and generating a SAS70 report. However, clients must validate not only that their service provider's report is unqualified with no serious exposures being identified but that the controls in the report reflect controls on processes that are acceptable to their own SOX auditors. Their SOX auditors should be able to use the SAS70 report in lieu of conducting their own audit so that they can attest to management's assessment of installation and effectiveness of operation controls during a specified time period. After all, the client is the one with accountability for compliance, and the SAS70 report might help him or her feel comfortable that all of their processes are in compliance, even if they have been outsourced.

The benefit to the service provider is that they can effectively compete with other outsourcing service providers if they can demonstrate that the controls used within their processes having been accepted by independent outside auditors. Asking their outside auditors to conduct SAS70 audits can be expensive for them, but can result in additional future sales to service providers. Potential client companies can obtain an increased comfort level that they will pass a SOX audit and that their processes are well controlled if they receive SAS70 reports from their service providers.

After a client consults with their external audit firm and service provider they can make a decision as to whether or not to request a SAS70 report. This is not always an easy decision; all of the pros and cons and business effects should be reviewed before that decision is made.